the
naked
FOODS
cookbook

THE WHOLE-FOODS, HEALTHY-FATS, GLUTEN-FREE GUIDE TO LOSING WEIGHT & FEELING GREAT

margaret floyd | james barry

New Harbinger Publications, Inc.

Publisher's Note

This publication is designed to provide accurate and authoritative information in regard to the subject matter covered. It is sold with the understanding that the publisher is not engaged in rendering psychological, financial, legal, or other professional services. If expert assistance or counseling is needed, the services of a competent professional should be sought.

Distributed in Canada by Raincoast Books

Copyright © 2012 by Margaret Floyd and James Barry
New Harbinger Publications, Inc.
5674 Shattuck Avenue
Oakland, CA 94609
www.newharbinger.com

Photographs by Jasmine Lord
Cover design by Amy Shoup
Text design by Michele Waters-Kermes
Acquired by Catharine Meyers
Edited by Marisa Solis

7/12 $21.95

Library of Congress Cataloging-in-Publication Data

Floyd, Margaret.
   The naked foods cookbook : easy, unprocessed, gluten-free, full-fat recipes for losing weight and feeling great / Margaret Floyd and James Barry.
      p. cm.
   Includes bibliographical references.
   ISBN 978-1-60882-318-5 (pbk.) -- ISBN 978-1-60882-319-2 (pdf e-book) -- ISBN 978-1-60882-320-8 (epub)
   1. Cooking (Natural foods) 2. Natural foods. 3. Nutrition. 4. Health. 5. Weight loss. 6. Low-fat diet. I. Barry, James, 1973- II. Title.
   TX741.F48 2012
   641.3'02--dc23

                          2011044073

Printed in the United States of America

14   13   12

10   9   8   7   6   5   4   3   2

For those who dedicate their lives to growing food

Contents

List of Recipes

SALADS AND SIDES

SAUCES, DRESSINGS, AND DIPS

SOUPS AND STEWS

ENTRÉES

SWEET AND SAVORY SNACKS

DESSERTS

Acknowledgments

We are so grateful to be able to follow up Margaret's book *Eat Naked* with a complete book of recipes. We are equally fortunate to have had so much support in the form of family, friends, and colleagues. And away we go...

We could not have finished this book on time without the gracious assistance of our recipe testers: Andrea Butler-Barry, Caren Rich, and Debra Joy. These recipes would not have achieved their potential without your thorough notes.

A big thank-you to Caroline Barringer for reviewing the "Better Than Naked" chapter. Caroline is an expert in her field, and we were fortunate enough to meet her while taking her Certified Healing Food Specialist Training Course. She is a true friend, and we are so grateful for her support and guidance.

Loretta Barrett, our literary agent, inadvertently became one of our food testers when we invited her over for dinner. Loretta, your guidance and counsel are priceless. We consider ourselves very lucky to be working with the best in the business.

Thank you to the amazing team at New Harbinger for making the process such a breeze. Thank you for the opportunity to share these recipes and the naked philosophy with the world. Your support and faith in both *Eat Naked* and *The Naked Foods Cookbook* are inspiring.

Thank you to Stephanie Shearer, Sheree Gillaspie, and Jorge Gonzalez for your recipe contributions. *The Naked Foods Cookbook* is that much better due to you. Thank you for trusting us with your recipes.

Our tireless and wonderful photographer, Jasmine Lord, did an exceptional job capturing the spirit of our food and cooking techniques visually. This book wouldn't have been what it is without her incredible work. And a big thank-you to our friends Mark Smith and the Murray family, who let us take over their kitchens for various photo and video shoots.

We've gotten a lot of support over the years from clients of both Margaret's nutrition practice and James's meal-delivery service, Wholesome2Go. Thank you for your questions and insights. So much of your feedback helped inform the recipes in this book.

Many friends and family members sampled and gave us feedback on the naked foods we made. We get so much pleasure from nurturing those around us. Thank you for receiving our gifts.

We've both been shaped and influenced by a multitude of people throughout our lives. Most important, our parents, whom we love dearly. Margaret credits her love of food to long afternoons at her grandmother's house, learning how to make the perfect piecrust and how to roast a chicken. James would not be a chef today if it weren't for the influence of four people: his mom, Carol Barry, for teaching him to scramble an egg; his father, George Barry, for letting him copilot the backyard barbecues; Michael McDonald, for teaching him the joy of making meals from scratch; and his junior high culinary arts teacher, Marilee Dunn, for her nurturance and support of his passion for cooking.

Last, we want to thank the local farmers. While writing this book, we shopped every weekend for ingredients at the farmers markets in Mar Vista, Culver City, and Santa Monica. None of us would be able to eat naked without the work of small farms everywhere. We are indebted to your hard work and nourished by your beautiful food.

Introduction

Cooking holds a very special place in our hearts. Professionally, it's our primary focus. Personally, it changed the course of our lives. You see, we fell in love in the kitchen. It was probably inevitable. All those long, hot hours, perfecting delicious naked recipes for Margaret's first book, *Eat Naked: Unprocessed, Unpolluted, and Undressed Eating for a Healthier, Sexier You*. All that talk of food, flavor, and vibrant health. With a shared passion for something so life giving and sensual, how could we resist each other?

As humans, we're biologically wired to avoid pain and seek pleasure. Feeding ourselves is one of the wonderful ways we get to give ourselves that pleasure multiple times a day, every single day. Sometimes in the general chaos of everyday life, this perspective gets lost. For many, eating is a hassle or a source of stress, a necessary evil that's time consuming, waist expanding, and, more times than not, very confusing.

Food preparation isn't just about fueling ourselves, ensuring proper macronutrient combination, or impressing the neighbors with our culinary talents. Cooking is about deep nourishment on every level: physical, emotional, and, for some, even spiritual. When we prepare our own food, we're able to infuse it with love and the intention to nourish. As sentimental as this may sound, that intention will affect the quality of the food and those lucky enough to eat it.

In *Eat Naked*, Margaret explained why many foods are unhealthy and the benefits of eating more naked foods. She got you started with a few recipes and some basic transition strategies for switching to a naked diet. In *The Naked Foods Cookbook*, we're going to take the *Eat Naked* principles and apply them in depth in your kitchen. Let's bring this stuff to life and rediscover the sensuality, pleasure, and deep nourishment we derive from food.

We have several goals for this book. First and foremost, we want to make healthy cooking accessible. There's a myth that healthy cooking takes loads of time to do from scratch. Well, that just isn't so. You don't have to live in the kitchen to have home-cooked meals. In fact, during busy weeks, we rarely take more than ten to fifteen minutes to prepare dinner, and we make almost all our meals at home. We'll show you ways of making the best use of your time in the kitchen.

We also want to prove that healthy cooking doesn't have to be bland, boring, and tasteless—it can be loaded with flavor and absolutely delicious. In addition, we've provided healthier options for foods that are often considered unhealthy or that are common guilty pleasures. We've made a strong commitment to showing that healthy food can be wonderfully appetizing.

Some other points:

- 100 percent of these recipes are gluten-free.

- We don't include caloric information because we don't believe that that is what's most important. In fact, counting calories shifts your attention away from the more important aspects of food—such as nutrient density, freshness, and quality—to a somewhat arbitrary number that portrays just one very small piece of the nutritional puzzle. If you're really intent on determining the caloric information for the recipes, there are plenty of online calculators that will help you do the math.

- Most of all, have fun with it. Cooking doesn't have to be work. Get creative with it! Turn on some tunes, throw on a sexy apron, and invite a guest or two over. Go on, put your naked self into these recipes. We've got your back.

PART 1

let's talk shop

1
Introduction to Eating Naked

Before you roll up your sleeves, throw on an apron, and get down to business, let's sort out a few details about what all this naked stuff is about.

If you haven't yet read Margaret's first book, *Eat Naked: Unprocessed, Unpolluted, and Undressed Eating for a Healthier, Sexier You*, this chapter will get you up to speed on what we mean by eating naked. For those of you who've already read *Eat Naked*, this chapter is a review of the basics, with some new ways of framing the conversation to make it even easier for you to identify naked food.

Eating naked is all about eating clean, whole, unprocessed food. This means food without all those unnecessary extras that expand our waistlines and damage our health, such as pesticides, additives, and preservatives; in other words, that long list of unpronounceable ingredients on food packaging.

Four simple questions can help you determine whether something is naked or not:

1. Where was the food grown or raised?

2. How was the food grown or raised?

3. What happened to the food from the time it was harvested until it reached my kitchen?

4. How was the food prepared?

Let's look at each of these in detail.

Where Was the Food Grown or Raised?

Key Principle: *The Closer It Originated to You, the More Naked It Is.*

You've likely heard that local produce is a good thing. It is, and that's because when it's local, it has usually been allowed to ripen before being picked, and thus has more nutritional value. Local food is often fresher since it didn't have to travel as far to get to you. This also means it feeds your local economy and doesn't have as much of an environmental footprint.

Now, if you live somewhere that has a prolonged growing season, obtaining local produce year-round is much easier than if you live somewhere with interminably cold winter months. That's okay. You can get healthy produce in a couple of ways. For one, frozen produce is a good alternative to fresh produce. Frozen produce is picked at the peak of season, when the produce is at its tastiest, and then flash-frozen very shortly after harvest. Depending

---

DIY Naked Food Storage—How to Make Your Seasonal Produce Last All Year

If you want to be as naked as possible and are looking for a do-it-yourself strategy to sustain yourself through the winter months on local produce, here are three things to try.

1. **Devise your own cold storage.** The goal of cold storage is to keep produce dormant. As such, temperature and humidity are key. Cold cellars or storage must be dark and ventilated. Note that fruits release ethylene, which speeds up the ripening process of vegetables, so the two should never be stored together.

2. **Freeze your own produce.** Freezing fruit and vegetables yourself can take a little work, but if it means you'll get your local produce even during the cold months, it's well worth the effort. Check our resource page on www.eatnakednow.com for a step-by-step guide to freezing your own vegetables.

3. **Culture your fruits and vegetables.** Culturing is a natural preservation technique that not only preserves the food but also enhances its nutritional value. This is different from canning, which uses heat that damages the delicate nutrients in the produce. The only exception to this is tomato, which has a nutrient called lycopene that is more bioavailable when the tomatoes have been cooked. Natural culturing uses beneficial bacteria, which eat up many of the sugars in the fruit or vegetable, to create lactic acid, which then preserves the food. No heat is applied, and the process adds loads of enzymes and probiotics, and increases the content of some vitamins. We explain more about culturing in chapter 4, "Better Than Naked Food-Preparation Techniques," and we've included many recipes that use these techniques in the recipe section.

on your location and the time of year, sometimes (and somewhat counterintuitively) frozen produce is actually the better choice. Freezing is one of the easiest and least damaging ways of preserving food, and, when done just after harvest, it preserves most of the nutritional value. The key is to find frozen produce that is just the produce, without sauces or flavorings. That's where the un-naked "overdressed" stuff creeps in.

If the frozen food aisle leaves you wanting, don't sweat it. Some types of food fare really well in cold storage and so can be found throughout the off-season. And if you need to buy produce that was shipped from far away, so be it. It's not the end of the world. Ultimately, it's far more important that you eat the produce regardless of its origin.

So far, we've been talking only about produce, but eating locally spans all types of food. Don't forget your local egg, dairy, and meat farmers, especially the smaller ones specializing in pastured poultry and eggs, grass-fed beef and dairy, and pasture-fed pork. Many farmers are now selling their naked meat and eggs at farmers markets, and so these delicious, nutrient-dense foods are becoming even more accessible and easy to find.

How Was the Food Grown or Raised?

Key Principle: *The More It Was Grown in Harmony with Its Natural Environment, the More Naked It Is.*

The next question to ask is *how* the food was grown or raised. The most naked food is grown in harmony with its natural environment without any synthetic chemicals, hormones, or antibiotics. In the case of anything plant-based, such as produce, grains, nuts, beans, and seeds, this means grown organically or, even better, biodynamically. Like organic farming, biodynamic farming doesn't use any synthetic fertilizers, herbicides, or pesticides. Biodynamic agriculture takes organic agriculture a step further, recognizing and using the interconnectivity between the earth, plants, animals, humans, and the cosmos. It's often described as "beyond organic" because it makes extensive use of specific farming techniques such as including fermented additives in compost, and planting and harvesting crops according to the lunar calendar. This means you're getting food that was truly grown in harmony with Mother Nature and Her natural cycles.

If you're not able to find biodynamic food, certified organic is your next best bet. Certified organic means that an independent third party determined no synthetic chemicals were used to grow the food. There have been some complaints against industrial organic agriculture, since it still relies heavily on monocrops, which lead to soil erosion and are resource-intensive, but it's much more widely available than biodynamic produce.

When it comes to animal products—meat, dairy, fish, eggs, or any fats of animal origin—the most important consideration is how the animals involved are raised and fed. Naked animal products come from animals raised humanely in environments that allow them to engage in their own natural behaviors and eat what they are biologically designed to eat. This means cows grazing on grass, chickens allowed out on pasture to roam and peck for grubs and insects, and pigs allowed to root and scavenge. In many ways, these criteria are far more important than whether an animal product is organic or not.

When it comes to animal products, "organic" simply refers to the feed and what, if anything, the animal should be treated with should it become sick. There are also requirements for access to the outdoors, but they are minimal. In many cases, being organic doesn't mean the feed is based on what the animal was biologically designed to eat. For example, in the case of cows—ruminants that eat grass—the "organic" label may mean they were fed organic corn and soy, not the grass their stomachs were designed to handle. It's more important that the cow eat grass than that the feed be organic yet inappropriate for the animal to begin with.

That said, if you're not able to find grass-fed beef or pastured chicken or pork, organic is the next most naked option. We recommend that you steer clear entirely of any animal product that doesn't have this as its minimum standard.

A Note about Raw Milk

Raw milk is milk that hasn't been pasteurized. The heat of pasteurization destroys bacteria—both the good and the bad—along with delicate enzymes and several other important nutrients. When milk comes from cows fed grain, raised in industrial feedlots, and milked in unsanitary dairies, pasteurization is critically important. But when milk comes from cows living on pasture, eating grass, and part of small-scale and highly sanitary dairies pasteurization isn't as necessary. We drink raw milk from grass-fed cows since it's the most naked of all dairy products, and you'll see several of the recipes call for it. If you choose to drink raw milk, the quality of the milk, the health of the animal it came from, and the cleanliness of the dairy are of paramount importance. Be safe and do your homework before consuming it.

If you're interested in the topic of raw milk, see the "Resource" section at www.eatnakednow.com or the discussion of naked dairy in *Eat Naked*.

What Happened to the Food from Harvest to My Kitchen?

Key Principle: *The Closer It Is to Its Original State, the More Naked It Is.*

When we're talking about naked food, this question is without doubt the most important. What happened to that food from the time it was harvested until it arrived in your kitchen? Naked food has had as little done to it as possible. It's as close to its original form as you can get.

So much of the damage we do to our food happens at this stage in the process. This is when we take a food—whole and perfect, just as nature intended—and turn it into a food product. During this process, the whole food is broken down into its individual nutritional components, rearranged, modified, or somehow altered, and then reconstituted into something that's got a long shelf life, that's in a grab-and-go convenient package, or that's some kind of new, nifty food product marketed to one of our hot buttons: convenience or the latest dietary fad. It's a process of disassembling, rearranging, and reassembling nutrients into a nutritionally compromised version of the original.

The details of this process look different from food to food, but there are some common factors. Inevitably, the nutritional integrity of the food is compromised. After processing, it's a lesser-than version of the original. Often artificial and unnatural ingredients are added to preserve, enhance, or stabilize this new food product. Food processors add colorings, "natural" or artificial flavors, stabilizers, emulsifiers, and synthetic replacements for nutrients lost or damaged in processing.

The health impact of these additives ranges from neutral to toxic, depending on the additive. What's perhaps most disturbing is that the impacts of these various additives are always studied in isolation, but that's not how we consume them. We eat them in combination, as additive cocktails the synergistic effect of which we have never studied. Certainly no one is suffering from an additive deficiency.

But it's not just what we're adding to food during processing, it's what we're taking away. We are just beginning to recognize the importance of cofactors on how nutrients function in our bodies. For example, vitamin D is a fat-soluble vitamin. Your body needs both the vitamin and fat, a cofactor, in order to properly digest and absorb it. As you might imagine, those foods containing vitamin D often also contain the fat required for its assimilation. Milk is a good example of this: In its whole, unprocessed state, it includes both vitamin D and fat. But, in our fat-phobic ways, we often remove the very fat that's needed for our bodies to access the vitamin. Skim milk and other low- or nonfat dairy products are a great example of food processing whereby we've removed important nutrients that are required for the full bioavailability of the food.

The moral of the story? Naked food is left whole and unrefined. This means that even if we don't fully understand the multitude of cofactors at work (and we don't), chances are Mother Nature provided everything needed within the food in its whole form. This also means that we don't need to worry about whether all those extras added into processed foods are hurting us or not. Leave them out and there's nothing to worry about.

How Was the Food Prepared?

Key Principle: *The Less We Do to It, the More Naked It Is.*

With only a few exceptions, everything we do to food from the time it's harvested until it reaches our plates damages its nutritional integrity. Even something as simple as chopping speeds up the breakdown of the food and reduces its nutritional content.

Now, does this mean we need to eat everything raw? No, not at all, although we will concede that just about everyone could benefit from more raw foods in their diet. What this means is that naked food is prepared minimally, leaving as much of that natural goodness in the food as possible. The less we do to it, the better. This is good news for the busy types out there, because it means less time in the kitchen and more time actually enjoying the food. We'll go into this in detail in chapter 3, "Naked Cooking Techniques."

Still confused about what's the most naked version of a particular food? We've included an appendix with tables from *Eat Naked* that summarize the basic guidelines for eating naked for each food type. For an even deeper discussion of the particulars, we recommend that you pick up your very own copy of *Eat Naked* or visit www.eatnakednow.com for lots of free articles exploring the different aspects of eating naked.

2

In the Naked Kitchen

If you're like us, then you know: If it's in the kitchen, you'll eat it. Take a look at your kitchen in its current state. Open the cupboards. What do you see? Are there rows of cans, packaged foods, bags of chips, soda pop? Now open the refrigerator and freezer. Are there microwave dinners, cartons of skim milk, margarine?

Now imagine your kitchen naked. A naked kitchen isn't bare or boring—it's alive. A bowl of fresh fruit on the table, nuts soaking in glass jars on the counter, a pot of broth brewing on the stove. There's a window box with fresh herbs growing in it, ready to be trimmed and added to your naked meals.

Opening the cupboards reveals rows of glass jars filled with a variety of whole grains, beans, nuts, and seeds. The only cans you have are ones that contain ingredients like whole coconut milk.

The fridge is bursting with fruit and veggies. A carton of pastured eggs from the farmers market, some homemade condiments, and cultured butter rest in the door. Covered glass dishes with last night's leftovers sit on the shelf, alongside some raw milk and a few homemade sauces and dressings.

This is an active kitchen. There's no hint of a TV dinner here; in fact, there's not a microwave to heat one if you wanted to. It feels clean, abundant, and light. The fresh smells emanating from it are nourishing and inspiring.

Sound idyllic? It is. Sound difficult to set up? It's actually not that hard. Much of it is an exercise in simplifying. Let's look at some of the basics.

The Refrigerator

Your fridge is the center point of your naked kitchen. Eating naked means eating fresh foods, which means having the proper refrigeration system to store all that natural goodness.

If you're lucky enough to have the opportunity to choose a new refrigerator, then choose a naked fridge—an energy-efficient model with the freezer on the bottom (we never did understand the logic of the freezer on top, since heat rises). Remember, naked isn't just about food, it's also about healthy living and sustainability. Of course, you can make do with what you have as well.

A naked fridge is also a clean fridge. It's important to clean your fridge at least once every two weeks. We use a 10 to 1 mixture of water to rubbing alcohol as a natural sanitizer.

The magic temperature for your refrigerator is 38°F. This is the temperature at which food will last the longest without danger of freezing and at which most bugs and bacteria can't survive. Fridges have temperature dial settings but most don't have gauges showing the actual temperature. Opening and closing your fridge door causes the front of the fridge to be warmer than the back. For this reason, store anything that's highly perishable at the back of the fridge. You can also buy a small thermometer that attaches to the inside of your fridge to ensure that it's a maximum of 38°F. Thermometers designed for wine cellars work well for this purpose. You may have to adjust the temperature dial a few times until you find the right setting.

Fridge Door Essentials

- **Tamari gluten-free soy sauce** (the naked version of soy sauce)

- **Miso paste** (great for soups and dressings—there are several varieties and they all taste different, so try a different one each time until you find the kind you like)

- Store-bought or homemade **Cultured Butter** (page 64), ideally from grass-fed cows (not margarine or any other butter substitute)

- Store-bought or homemade basic grain or Dijon **Mustard** (page 67), made with only naked ingredients and no sugar

- Delicate unrefined **seed oils** (toasted/untoasted sesame oil, hemp seed oil, pumpkin seed oil, flaxseed oil)

- **Maple syrup** (grade B or C, for maximum nutrient content)

- **Vinegar** (apple cider, balsamic, brown rice)

- **Nuts and seeds** (the oil in nuts and seeds will cause them to go rancid over time; if you're eating them infrequently, store them in the fridge for lasting freshness)

Things that don't need to be refrigerated: ghee, lard, basil, garlic, onions, potatoes, olive oil, coconut oil, and honey. Best to keep these items in a dark, cold cabinet.

Stocking the Naked Fridge

Start with the largest shelf, the one that normally has ready-made canned drinks, soda pop, and cartons of juice. Replace these overly processed drinks with a couple of big pitchers, one with some homemade iced tea and another with water infused with cucumber and mint (fill a pitcher with filtered water and add four slices of cucumber, two slices of lime, and a couple sprigs of mint—voilà!). If you choose, have a bottle or two of mineral water on hand, and, if you have access to raw dairy and like it, a quart of raw milk.

Smaller shelves will be for leftovers, sauces, cultured veggies, and other such products. It's also good practice to keep flours in an airtight container in the fridge. Once grains are milled into flour their nutritional life shortens. Keeping them in your fridge will help them stay fresh longer. Also in the fridge, store your fresh herbs and asparagus in similar fashion to flowers: stem side down in a jar with enough water to immerse the bottom where they've been cut. Use a drawer for cheese and meat. Keep these products well sealed and separate from your produce and fruits.

Produce keeps longest unwashed and uncut. Any bins or shelves holding produce should be lined with a clean cloth or unbleached paper towel. If there's enough room, keep fruit separate from vegetables. Fruit is best with the heavier, harder fruits on the bottom and tender fruits like peaches at the top. To make berries last longer, put them in a single layer on a plate with a clean paper towel, uncovered. Don't leave your fruits or vegetables in the thin, flimsy bags you got from the grocery store. These bags trap moisture, which increases spoilage. If the produce is in the crisper drawer, it doesn't need to have a bag, but produce left on the shelves will last longer in a thick, resealable bag with a dry, unbleached paper towel to absorb condensation. Before sealing the bag, push as much air out of it as possible.

The foundation of any naked meal is an abundance of vegetables, so fill the bottom drawers and shelves with fresh vegetables and fruit. Yet, it's also important to be able to see what you have so you can get creative about how you want to combine it all. Buy only enough fresh produce to last you one week.

The naked fridge doesn't have a lot of condiments or store-bought dressings and sauces. Those that are

Produce Every Naked Fridge Should Have in Stock

- **Salad greens** (eating at least one mostly raw meal daily is optimal; salads are an easy way to do this)

- **Dark leafy greens** (chard, kale, collards, cabbages, bok choy, spinach, broccoli—mix it up, you choose)

- "Snackable" **veggies** (cucumber, bell peppers, celery, carrots, snap peas, zucchini—anything that's easy to munch on)

- A few **lemons and limes** (these will come in handy with your mineral water and add a *ka-pow* to your meals and dressings)

store bought have few ingredients, all of which are recognizable. The fridge door is a great place for your homemade dressings, perishable oils, butter, miso pastes, and condiments (see sidebar, "Fridge Door Essentials").

The freezer might be your biggest challenge. Many of us have items in our freezers we can't even recognize anymore from all the frost buildup. Get rid of all those prepackaged frozen meals. It's time to restock your freezer with your own, naked foods. Buy a bunch of bananas, peel them, and place them in a sealed container for smoothies or a sweet-treat alternative to ice cream. Frozen berries and certain vegetables like peas, corn, and green beans are picked at their peak season and flash-frozen to be eaten off-season. As long as these items have no added ingredients or preservatives, these are perfectly acceptable naked foods. Also stow fresh ginger in your freezer in a plastic bag to keep it fresh longer and make it easier to grate.

If you're not a vegetarian, you'll also have some frozen meat: maybe a whole, pastured chicken, grass-fed beef, some fish. If you have the space for it and can make the investment, buy a separate freezer unit that can be kept in a basement or garage and is big enough to hold large quantities of meat. Naked meats can be pricier, and the most cost-effective way to buy naked meat is in large quantities like a quarter or half cow. Your freezer is a great place to store your meat, which is easily perishable.

Stove, Oven, and Toaster Oven

When cooking in a naked kitchen, we use the stovetop, an oven, or a toaster oven. No microwave. Microwaves use electromagnetic energy to create molecular friction, heating food from the inside out, which is the opposite of how a stove, oven, grill, or fire would cook it. Several studies have shown that microwaving food causes a significantly higher proportion of antioxidants and vitamins to be lost, and negatively affects proteins. This happens even if you're just reheating a meal that was previously cooked (Vallejo et al. 2003; Pitchford 2002).

Ultimately, it doesn't take that much more time to reheat last night's dinner in a small saucepan on the stove or on a tray in the oven, and the nutritional benefits far outweigh the convenience factor. Turn the oven to 395°F and put the empty tray in the oven for 5 to 10 minutes to preheat it. Put the food on the hot oven tray, and reheating your food will take only about 5 minutes.

If you're in the market for a new stove, pick one that fits your needs best. The two basic categories are electric and gas, with many choices in each. We prefer gas stoves because they heat up quickly and the temperature is easily adjusted, cooking things evenly and predictably. Electric induction stoves are easy to clean and heat with extreme precision. There are pros and cons to both, so do your research and find what works best for your space. We don't recommend the coil-element electrical stovetop. They heat up and cool down slowly, the temperature settings aren't accurate, and they use a lot of electricity.

A toaster oven is a good compromise between heating your whole oven (which isn't all that energy efficient) and using a microwave oven. The toaster oven heats up quickly and takes up even less space than a microwave. Convection ovens and convection toaster ovens use a fan to distribute heat within the unit more evenly, speeding up cooking time at lower temperatures. The fans allow the hot air to reach foods on all rack levels evenly.

The Naked Pantry

Your pantry is where you store nonperishable ingredients. The naked pantry has no prepared canned or packaged meals. Here you'll find jars of dried beans, grains, nuts, and seeds. This is also where you store your dried seaweeds, chiles, and other dried spices and herbs.

You want your pantry to be dark and cold. Don't use doorless cabinets or kitchen closets with heating vents. Light and heat can affect your stored items like extra-virgin olive oil and other items like potatoes, onions, and garlic. If you use generic jars or bins, label them with the name of the contents and the purchase date. If you're using a see-through container, cut the name from the packaging of the food you're storing and place that visibly in the container. When you refill a container that's not completely empty, don't put new on top of old. First empty the old contents into a bowl, then pour in the new contents and put the old back on top. This reduces waste and ensures your supplies will never be stale or old.

The Naked Spice Rack

It's best to buy unground spices. Similar to flours, once spices are ground they start to lose their potency. Buy a small coffee grinder, but instead of using it for coffee use it exclusively for your spices. Clean it between uses with a lightly dampened towel. Follow the manufacturer's directions closely for safe and proper care. Not only are spices more naked when they're freshly ground, their flavors will be far more vibrant. Nothing beats freshly ground spices. To increase their fragrance even further, put the whole seeds in a dry skillet and lightly toast them over medium heat. Once the potent fragrance reaches your nose (about 2 minutes or less), pull the pan off the heat and grind the seeds or pods to add to your meal of choice.

Cupboards and Countertops

When it comes to cupboards and countertops, clean and uncluttered is the name of the game. A clean environment is inspirational and allows for creativity. You want to be able to move around freely, make a bit of a mess, and then clean up easily.

Keep dishes and cups you use frequently within easy reach. Keep appliances in the cupboard or on a shelf, not on your countertop. In our household, the dish rack is the only item always out. Leaving dishes to dry on a rack takes far less time than towel drying, so we take the easier route. There's also a big bowl with fresh fruit on the table. Next to the stove we keep a utensil holder with the tools we use most frequently when cooking (see list of basic kitchen tools below), but otherwise, the counters are bare.

One thing that's notably absent is the set of oils and spices that some people like to store next to, or even on a shelf above, the stove. This is a big no-no for a naked kitchen. Oils are very delicate, and constant exposure to sunlight and heat will damage them.

When Cans Make Sense*

Sometimes canned foods make their way into the naked pantry, and if they don't have unnecessary additives or sweeteners, this can be okay. Foods you'll find in our naked pantry:

- Coconut milk (look for a brand with just coconut milk, water, and maybe guar gum for emulsification as ingredients)

- Canned tomatoes (whole or other) and tomato paste

- Canned fish: tuna, wild salmon, sardines, anchovies

- Canned beans, ideally without added salt

*Note: Frederick vom Saal, PhD, an endocrinologist at the University of Missouri, published findings that the resin linings of food and beverage cans contain bisphenol-A (BPA), a synthetic estrogen that has been linked to ailments ranging from reproductive problems to heart disease, diabetes, and obesity (Vom Saal 2009). Acidity in many canned products (tomatoes, beans, and soda) causes BPA to leach into the food. This is more dangerous to developing children and unhealthy individuals than to healthy adults. The ideal solution is to not buy *any* canned items. In the case of tomatoes, this is not an option when tomatoes are not in season and you want to make a naked recipe using tomatoes. We have taken the stance that the benefits of cooked tomatoes outweigh the risks. If possible, buy cooked tomatoes in glass bottles (which do not have resin linings) from companies like Bionaturae and Coluccio or in Tetra Paks from brands like Pomì. Otherwise, just limit your intake of any canned food and eat most of your food naked.

Basic Kitchen Tools

Here's a list of the supplies every kitchen needs. If you have only this gear, you'll go far and you'll be able to make everything in this book.

- Three to four cutting boards of different sizes. You want to have a different board for raw meat, cooked meat, and produce, so make sure you've got at least three.

- Three good, well-sharpened knives. Save your money and don't buy the whole knife set. Most of them just sit in their nice little knife block and gather dust. The three knives you really need are an 8- to 10-inch chef's knife, a paring knife, and a serrated knife. Make sure you also get a steel for honing the knife.

- A veggie peeler. Find one that works well. Bad veggie peelers are nightmarishly difficult to work with.

- A big utensil holder next to your stove that's stocked with a heat-resistant spatula for mixing, a set of tongs, a flat metal spatula for flipping, a slotted spoon, a whisk, and a ladle. No wooden or low-grade plastic spoons (these wear down over time, and bacteria can get into the cracks and crevices, making them difficult to clean properly). We recommend stainless steel or high-grade, heat-resistant plastic.

- A grater. Ideally one of those block graters that has four different sides and types of grates. If you're feeling fancy, you can also get a zester, but most four-sided graters have a zesting side.

- A set of copper or stainless steel pans. Much like knives, you don't need to get a full set. One small, one medium, and one large saucepan, one small and one large skillet, and one large stockpot are truly all you'll need. If you're going to invest in your kitchen, this is where to spend a little money. Stay away from the nonstick variety. The coating that makes it nonstick is very delicate and toxic. It scratches and flakes easily, so it's easy to get it in your food.

- A set of stainless steel or glass bowls of all sizes. We prefer stainless steel because they're lighter and easier to work with.

- Stainless steel or aluminum half-oven trays (full size is usually too big for a home oven). If using the cheaper aluminum trays, make sure to also line the tray with parchment paper so your food isn't touching the pan as it cooks. This also makes cleanup a cinch. You'll want at least two. We use them to reheat our leftovers.

- Clear heat-resistant glass dishes of all sizes with lids. These are imperative for food storage. While plastic containers are cheaper, heat-resistant glass containers last forever and can be put in the oven for reheating food. More important, they don't leach anything into the food, nor do they absorb colors or smells like plastic does. Another bonus is the nice visual aesthetic of the containers, and the clear glass allows you to see what's inside without having to open it.

- A set of mason jars of various sizes. Mason jars are great for storing both dried and wet foods. Our cupboards are lined with jars of grains, nuts, and seeds, and we use the jars for storing leftover soups and sauces. If you want to get fancy, buy a labeler to create matching labels on all your jars.

- A citrus juicer. We're not talking about a big machine. Just the small citrus juicer (hand held or cup-style) that will help you squeeze that goodness out of lemons and limes. You'll get more juice for your squeeze compared to squeezing by hand with a fork.

- A lettuce spinner. Cleaning lettuce from the farmers market is a breeze if you have a lettuce spinner but a pain if you don't. Lettuce spinners also revitalize wilted greens.

- A colander, a small fine-mesh sieve, and a large conical fine-mesh sieve or chinois to strain your stocks.

- A small coffee grinder used exclusively for spices and herbs.

- A set of measuring spoons and cups. Quality doesn't apply here. Just keep it affordable and simple. These are a necessity if you're baking and for those who like to be precise with their measurements. If neither applies to you, then feel free to skip these.

- A meat thermometer. This is the safest and easiest way to determine when meat has been cooked to the desired amount.

- A blender for making sauces, dressings, and smoothies. If you don't own one yet, see our recommendations in the Advanced Kitchen Tools section below.

- A food processor, the ultimate in making big things small in a hurry. Consider this appliance your hired hand. It chops, dices, grates, blends, and purées. Use it when making cultured veggies, dips like pesto and hummus, and flours from nuts.

Optional Advanced Kitchen Tools

If you're just getting reacquainted with your kitchen, you might want to flag this section to come back to later, after your new naked kitchen is in full swing. With the exception of the mandoline and scale, these gadgets involve a small investment ($150 to $500). While they're not absolutely necessary, they will certainly make your life in the kitchen much easier.

Mandoline

A mandoline is a tool for slicing and cutting foods. It makes julienne-style chopping and thin slicing a breeze. It's not a mandatory piece of kitchen equipment, but it will make your life much easier and reduce preparation time, especially for some of the fancier recipes we've included. We've indicated in the individual recipes which ones would benefit from this tool.

Digital Scale

Consider a digital scale, if you want to get fancy. Sometimes volume isn't the best gauge of measuring amounts. We assume most people don't have a scale, so you won't need one for this recipe book. However, we recommend weighing ingredients for precision recipes as you expand your culinary skills. You don't have to spend your whole paycheck on high-end equipment. Look for a flex scale that has a tare function for zeroing out weight.

High-Speed, High-Powered Professional Blender

Blenders aren't just for smoothies anymore. We use our blender to make sauces, dressings, frozen treats, soups, purées, raw-veggie smoothies…the list goes on. This is a worthy investment, and the right brand could last you a lifetime. Don't skimp on this item. Check out www.eatnakednow.com for some suggested brands. For a couple of foodies and health nuts like us, the phrase "this blender changed my life" wouldn't be an exaggeration.

The key difference between your average blender and a high-speed, high-powered professional blender can be summarized in one word: pulverize. This is something your standard blender simply cannot do. While it can crush, blend, and mix really well, it cannot *pulverize*. A high-powered blender not only makes big things small, it liquefies them.

Food Dehydrator

In chapter 4, "Better Than Naked Food-Preparation Techniques," we explain how soaking and/or sprouting nuts, seeds, grains, and beans is important to improve digestibility. Soaked nuts and seeds are healthier but aren't always as tasty as crispy nuts. A dehydrator can fix that by bringing your soaked nuts back to their original crunchy state without compromising their nutritional value the way roasting them does.

A dehydrator is a great appliance for making raw foods, enzyme-rich fruit leathers, dried fruits, and dried tomatoes. It's not an essential appliance, but if you've got the budget and the shelf space, it sure is a nice addition to a naked kitchen.

A Good Water Filtration System

Clean, unchlorinated water without any impurities is an important asset in the naked kitchen. Not only is it cleaner and healthier, it tastes better! Make sure that your system either remineralizes the water or doesn't filter it to pure H_2O, which is difficult for your body to absorb and can leach minerals from your bones and teeth over time.

Juicer

With the right blender, a juicer isn't totally necessary—it becomes just a different way to get your nutrients from whole foods. But as a supplement to your average blender, it can be a meal game-changer. A good juicer doesn't heat your foods, thus maintaining the enzymes. Masticating juicers can make nut and seed butters, and fiber-free juices, from items like wheatgrass and ginger. Juicers don't fit the "keepin' it easy" profile we typically endorse. They are tough to clean, heavy, and bulky. However, for the right household, they are a great addition.

Does your kitchen look very different from what we've outlined here? That's okay. Just take it one step at a time. For instance, start with a recipe or two of ours that you find compelling, and purchase the proper tools and ingredients as needed. You can do a big kitchen cleanout a little later on once you've got a few recipes under your belt and have a sense of some of the typical ingredients, systems, and patterns of this kind of cooking.

3

Naked Cooking Techniques

Many people don't take the time to read the hows and the whys of cooking, so given that you're reading this chapter, you're officially ahead of the game. Technique is underrated, but it makes all the difference between a so-so meal and wowing your family and friends.

When we first started collaborating in the kitchen, Margaret thought she was a pretty savvy, if untrained, cook. In fact, she was pretty sure she'd impress the pants off of James with her innovative recipe ideas and speedy tips. How quickly she was humbled. By simply cutting vegetables differently or taking the time to lightly roast a grain before cooking it, James transformed simple but (she soon realized) boring meals she'd made for years into tasty splendors.

Take a little time to play with the tips and techniques we've described here. Check out www.eatnakednow.com/videos for video clips that complement each section, if you're more of a visual learner. And remember, don't be intimidated. Mistakes are an important part of the cooking journey, so go make some!

Knife Skills

How to use a knife depends on the type of knife you're using. If you have a French chef's knife (the large knife with the sharp point), you want to keep the tip stationary on the cutting board and use the natural curve of the blade to chop in a rocking motion. Knives without tips require a different motion. With a cleaver you actually use your wrist in a karate-chopping motion while holding the knife. With a serrated knife, use a sawing motion. Whichever knife you choose, practice chopping slowly and comfortably with a relaxed wrist and shoulder.

The techniques below all assume you're using a standard chef's knife, unless we've indicated otherwise.

Chop—Chopping refers to cutting the food into similar-sized pieces. Perfection isn't important. Just approximate.

Mince—Mincing is chopping something finely. Basically, you make many passes at the food with your knife until it's in really small bits. Most mincing is used for herbs and garlic. Make sure when mincing that all the herbs are dry and that your knife is sharp. Dull knives crush the herbs instead of cutting them, leaving you with a pulpy mess.

Dice—Dicing means chopping something into a cube, but here we aren't so concerned with the shape, more the size. In this book we specify three sizes of dicing. A small dice is approximately ¼ inch, a medium dice is ½ inch, and a large dice is ¾ inch.

Peel—If you've got a steady hand, you can peel using a knife, but if you want to save time, use a peeler. For best control, peel toward yourself. The little notch on the side of the peeler can be used to dig out nubs in veggies like potatoes.

Julienne or Stick—Julienne is just a fancy word for really thin rectangular sticks or slices. When you want vegetables to cook quickly, this cut is a winner. A stick is a slightly larger, thicker version of the julienne, but you don't need to get picky here.

Shredding and Grating—Another way to speed up the cooking time of your vegetables is to grate them. Fibrous vegetables like cabbage are easier to chew and digest when finely shredded. Food processors make this quick work but require a few more steps for cleanup; graters and mandolines take a little more elbow grease but cleanup is a cinch.

Shapes (half moons, diagonals)—Half moons are made by cutting round produce—zucchini for example—in half lengthwise and then slicing those halves crosswise to your desired thickness. Cutting something on the diagonal means you cut the food at an angle, which exposes a greater surface of the vegetable and thus shortens the cooking time.

Time-Saving Strategy

Don't cut the end of the vegetable off. When dicing an onion, for example, first cut off a small piece so there's a flat surface. Place that side down. Then slice horizontally and vertically a few times just up to the end but not through it so that you have many sticks, still attached to the stem. Then use your hand to safely hold it all together and slice down on the vegetable. Voilà! You have created your diced vegetables with minimal effort. See the video demonstration of this and other knife skills at www.eatnakednow.com/videos.

Cooking Techniques

The number one question we are asked when we talk about cooking and eating naked is "Do you mean I have to eat everything raw?"

Good question. Cooking denatures food. That's the simple, if unfortunate, truth. It damages certain delicate nutrients and enzymes, and it can even create toxic by-products. That charcoal that makes barbecue so yummy? Carcinogenic. Bummer that it tastes so good.

That said, some people have difficulty digesting raw food. In fact, certain traditions, including many Asian traditions, emphasize cooked foods and limit raw foods. To complicate matters, some nutrients are actually brought out by heat. For example, the lycopene in tomatoes is more biologically available when the tomatoes have been cooked. But this is the exception, not the rule.

It's a good idea to have *some* raw foods every day. How much of your diet is raw and how much is cooked will depend to a large degree on your personal preference, on the strength of your digestive system, and on the climate and season. In the deep dark days of winter, you're unlikely to want a salad, and it's much more appropriate to have a nice warming bowl of soup.

The general principle with cooking is that the longer you cook something, the more nutritional value you cook out of the food. The less a food is cooked, the more naked it is. Here's a breakdown of the different ways of cooking food and their impact nutritionally.

Sautéing

Sautéing is done in a preheated frying pan over medium to medium-high heat. You want to hear a sizzle when you toss the food in the pan. The food will brown a little the longer you cook it. You can sauté with oils that are appropriate for higher heat, such as coconut oil, ghee, or lard, but water also works well.

Best for: Veggies, thinly sliced meats, quick-cooking shrimp.

Nutritional impact: Sautéing is best done quickly so that the veggies are still al dente. The less browned they are, the more the nutritional integrity of the food is preserved. You'll need to find that balance between cooked enough to be yummy and not so cooked that the food is "killed." Your green veggies should still be bright green. If they start to go pale, they're overdone.

Steaming

Steaming used to be the favorite of the health nuts. It is certainly the technique most often associated with stereotypically bland, tasteless health food. Many of our clients have sighed, "I hate steamed broccoli," when we encourage them to eat more greens. For this reason, we don't use steaming that often. Lightly sautéing works just as well and tastes better. Ultimately, it's difficult to infuse food with flavor when you steam it.

Steaming uses the steam from hot water or broth to cook the food. Unlike with boiling, the food doesn't touch the water. Most steaming is done in a steam basket. The food won't brown but can overcook quickly if left for too long.

Best for: Veggies, especially dark leafy greens such as collards, kale, and mustard greens.

Nutritional impact: Nutritionally speaking, lightly steaming your food is one of the best ways to preserve its nutritional value. But like any other cooking technique described here, if you overdo it, you kill the food.

Boiling

The opposite of steaming, boiling has a bad rap when it comes to healthy cooking. Images of soggy, pale vegetables, the life boiled completely out of them, come to mind. For this reason, we almost never use boiling for vegetables or meats, unless it's to start off a soup or stew, or is specific to the recipe, such as with Zesty Pulled Beef (page 194).

To boil something, bring a pot of water to a boiling point, add the food, and keep it there until the food is cooked through. Use a lid to help the water boil faster. Don't add salt to the water until it is already boiling. Salted water takes longer to boil.

Best for: Potatoes, grains, beans.

Nutritional impact: If used for vegetables and meat, boiling has a tendency to overcook your meal. It's much more appropriate for cooking starches like potatoes, grains, and beans, all of which need to be cooked thoroughly for optimum digestibility.

Grilling

Those crisscross char marks you see on the sizzling steaks in TV ads? They're the classic signature of grilled meat and appeal to the caveperson in us. Nutritionally speaking, grilling is one of the more harmful ways of cooking food, mostly because of our tendency to overdo it. Also, those char marks that taste so good are filled with heterocyclic amines (HCAs), which have been linked to cancer (Layton et al. 1995).

While it's not the best nutritionally, let's face it: Grilling is as American as apple pie and it's not going away any time soon. We recommend that you save it for special occasions and do it wisely. Grilling can be done on a barbecue grill or on a cast-iron stovetop grill. Whichever you use, allow the grill to get nice and hot before putting the food on it. You don't want to fiddle with the food once you've put it on the grill. Place it, then leave it untouched until it's ready to turn.

Best for: Meat, veggies, fish. Anything large enough to not fall through the grates.

Nutritional impact: The nutritional impacts of grilling depend on how much you cook the food and also on the equipment you use to cook it. For the least impact on your food, use the cast-iron stovetop grill. Outdoor barbecues cook with a much higher intensity of heat. When fat drips onto the hot coals, excess smoke is created, which surrounds and infuses the food with polycyclic aromatic hydrocarbons (PAHs). PAHs have been linked to cancer, reproductive challenges, and lung, liver, skin, and kidney damage (Wisconsin Department of Health and Family Services, 2000).

Citrus Searing (Cooking without Heat)

When you hear the word "sear" you probably think of quick cooking on high heat. That's one way of searing. But what we're talking about here is using juice from citrus fruits to "cook" the outside of the fish or meat, which is where pathogens in meat or fish live. Beef carpaccio from Italy is a common example of a dish prepared in this way. Citrus seared is one of the healthiest ways to eat meat protein, as the citrus kills off parasites and pathogens that might be present in the meat or fish, but leaves the nutritional integrity of the food intact. The longer the item is left in the citrus, the more it is "cooked." For instance, when making ceviche, a Spanish dish of citrus-seared fish or seafood, you want the fish cooked through, so you leave it in the citrus for up to several hours. If you just want a light outside searing, you'd want to take the fish out of the citrus within two hours. It's important when preparing meals using citrus searing that you use the highest-grade fish or meat.

Best for: Fish, meat. Can also be used for dark leafy greens such as kale.

Nutritional impact: Any heat-sensitive enzymes and nutrients are preserved, so you're getting the maximum nutritional value of the meat without the health- and nutrient-damaging effects of heat.

Broiling

When you broil, you use the oven with very high heat coming from above in close proximity to the food. It's a great technique for browning the tops of most things, but make sure to keep a keen eye on it, because we've burned more things this way than we'd like to admit.

Best for: Anything you want to brown quickly, such as frittatas.

Nutritional impact: When it comes to cooking anything in the oven, the nutritional impact depends on the level of heat. This makes broiling the most nutritionally damaging because it uses such high heat.

Baking and Roasting

When you bake, you use your oven with the heat coming from below, usually at medium heat, for longer periods of time. Roasting is similar to baking, just at a higher heat.

Best for: Baking: casseroles, slower-cooked dishes. Roasting: veggies—especially root veggies—meat, fish.

Nutritional impact: Once again, the higher the heat, the more damage done to the food. Baking is slightly less damaging than roasting.

Slow-Roasting and Dehydrating

If your oven's lowest temperature setting is below 200°F, you can use it for slow-roasting and dehydrating, which are basically the same thing, except that when you slow-roast you heat the food at a slightly higher temperature and thus do a little more damage. Set the oven at its lowest temperature and cook the food on an oven tray for up to several hours.

Best for: Nuts, fruit, vegetables, meat for jerky.

Nutritional impact: Of all the things you can use your oven for, slow-roasting and dehydrating do the least damage.

None of this is rocket science. We're using basic cooking techniques that you probably already know—we're just making sure we're doing them consciously and minimizing the damage to the food whenever possible. Now let's switch gears and look at food preparation techniques that actually *enhance* the nutritional value of the food.

Where's the Deep Fryer?

One of the techniques missing here is any kind of deep-frying. Deep-frying is the most damaging way to cook a food, as it involves heating large quantities of oils and fats to high temperatures and dropping foods in them to cook. While it's possible to minimize the negative impacts of deep-frying by using high-quality saturated fats only (the most stable and thus the least likely to go rancid from the heat), the high quantities of fat make this method of cooking something to be reserved for the rare special occasion.

4

Better Than Naked Food-Preparation Techniques

In the previous chapter we touched on the fact that there are different ways to prepare food, and almost everything we do to food depletes it nutritionally. From the moment it's harvested, its nutritional value begins to diminish. Even the act of chopping speeds its deterioration. For the most part, cooking naked is about minimizing what we do to food so that we're doing the least amount of damage.

"Better than naked" food-preparation techniques are the major exceptions to this rule. All three of the techniques we're going to share with you—soaking, sprouting, and culturing—not only preserve the nutritional value of the food, they enhance it.

Margaret briefly introduced the concept of "better than naked" foods in *Eat Naked*. Here we're going to look at each method in greater detail so that you clearly understand these techniques and how to incorporate them into your naked lifestyle.

Soaking

All grains, beans, nuts, and seeds are coated with antinutrients—enzyme inhibitors, phytates, and oxalates—for protection. Think about it: The biological purpose of that little grain of barley isn't to feed you, it's to create another plant. These metabolic inhibitors protect that grain from breaking down prematurely, giving it the best possible chance of producing another plant.

This is good news for the plant, but not for our bodies. Our digestive process is essentially a series of enzymes acting on the food to break it down. Enzyme inhibitors, as their name implies, make it much more difficult to break down the food. Phytates, which are natural insecticides, deplete our bodies of important minerals such as zinc, iron, and, to a lesser degree, calcium and magnesium. Oxalates, which prevent oxygen from penetrating, are key contributors to kidney stones. This is why we call these compounds "antinutrients"—instead of adding nutrients to our bodies, they deplete our bodies of them.

Soaking is the easiest way to neutralize these antinutrients. By soaking any grain, bean, nut, or seed in room-temperature water, you're basically tricking it into thinking it's about to be planted, and you're beginning the germination process. Basically, you're waking up the grain, bean, nut, or seed from dormancy. In germination, these antinutrients are removed and the predigestion of the grain, bean, nut, or seed has begun, making it far more absorbable to the body.

What Foods Need to Be Soaked?

All grains, beans, nuts, and seeds have these antinutrients, and most should be soaked. However, there are a few exceptions. Very small seeds, such as amaranth, chia, and flaxseeds, don't contain as many of these antinutrients and thus don't require soaking. In fact, if you soak flax or chia, you'll notice that the seeds break down too quickly and the water becomes gooey. Any other grain, bean, nut, or seed should be soaked if at all possible.

How to Soak Your Grains, Beans, Nuts, and Seeds

Soaking is the simplest of all the "better than naked" preparation techniques. All you need is the food you're going to soak, a jar or bowl, and some water (ideally filtered water). Simply put the grains, beans, nuts, or seeds into the jar or bowl (leaving enough room in the bowl for expansion), cover it generously with water, and let it sit at room temperature for 8 to 24 hours.

You'll notice that the grain, bean, nut, or seed will plump up significantly and the water will get a little cloudy. Drain the water, rinse the grains well, and then refrigerate them in a sealed container until you're ready to use them. They will last for about five days if kept cold.

Some Things You Can Do with Your Soaked Grains, Beans, Nuts, and Seeds

So now that you've soaked them, what do you do next?

- **Grains and beans**—If you're cooking them, prepare them as you would normally. For example, if you're cooking rice, soak it first, and then cook it as usual. You will need to reduce the amount of water you use slightly, as the grains will have absorbed some of the soaking water. If you're going to make them into flour for baking, you'll need a dehydrator or a low-heat convection oven to dry the grains first. Store the dried grains, not yet floured, in a sealed container in a cool, dry place until you need them for baking. Flour them only when you're ready to bake to keep them fresh. If you're storing them after flouring, store in a sealed container in the fridge to preserve maximum freshness.

- **Nuts and seeds**—Both nuts and seeds can be used just soaked, drained, and refrigerated, without cooking. As you'll see in several recipes in this book, we often use them to thicken smoothies, dressings, sauces, and desserts. You can also dehydrate them using a dehydrator, or slow-roast them on an oven tray at your oven's lowest temperature setting for 10 to 20 minutes. Stay close, as they can burn quickly if you're not paying attention.

- **Sprouting**—Soaking is the first step in sprouting any grain, bean, nut, or seed. See the next section for details.

31

Sprouting

Sprouting is the next step in the process of germination. When you sprout a grain, bean, nut, or seed, you wake up its enzymes, making it very alive and extremely nourishing. Sprouts are among the most nutrient dense of plant-based foods.

Sprouting isn't something that takes a lot of your time, just patience and consistency. Once you've done it a few times, you'll get into the rhythm of it and will find that it easily integrates into your daily routine. We typically have at least one or two things sprouting at all times. That means we've got a nice variety to use in salads and smoothies and to make raw versions of foods that would normally use cooked ingredients, such as hummus.

There are several different methods of sprouting. We've included the two primary ones we use here. You can buy automated sprouters, but either a sprouting bag or a mason jar with a mesh lid is really all you need. With only a few exceptions, you can sprout just about any grain, bean, nut, or seed. We're constantly sprouting new things. Last week we sprouted peanuts. This week we're sprouting fenugreek. Two weeks ago we sprouted garbanzo beans and mung beans. They've all got slightly different flavors and personalities. The most important things are that you use a high-quality (organic) grain, bean, nut, or seed, and that it's raw, dried, and unmodified (e.g., a whole-wheat berry is sproutable, but once it's been refined, it's not).

½ to 1 cup of the grain, bean, nut, or seed (for simplicity's sake, in this recipe we're going to refer to these collectively as "beans")

Filtered water

Soak the beans in a big bowl with at least 16 to 32 ounces filtered water overnight. You want the water to be 1 to 2 inches higher than the beans, as they'll expand as they absorb water.

In the morning, pour off the water and rinse the beans well in a colander or mesh strainer. Make sure the water is running clear—if it's murky, that's a sign either of a low-quality bean or that you need to rinse it again.

From here, you have options: to sprout using a mason jar or using a sprouting bag.

Method 1: Sprouting with a Mason Jar

Use a clean widemouthed quart-size mason jar. You can buy a special sprouting lid that is fitted with a mesh screen, or you can make one yourself by removing the lid from the ring, cutting some clean window screen material into a circle the same size as the lid, and then affixing the screen to the jar using the ring. This setup allows air to get in and water to get out. You can also use a cheesecloth instead of the window screen material, but you'll have to replace it daily, as it tends to get a bit moldy, which can affect the sprouting beans.

Put the soaked and rinsed beans in the bottom of the mason jar. Securely fasten the mesh lid on the jar, and fill the jar with filtered water. Then pour the water out. Set the jar in a dish rack or in a bowl, with the lid on the bottom and the jar leaning sideways so that the open end is exposed slightly to air. Remember: Air needs to be able to get in and water needs to be able to get out.

Rinse and drain the beans at least twice daily. The easiest way to schedule this is first thing in the morning when you get up and are making your breakfast, and last thing in the evening as you're doing the dinner dishes. Eventually a small tail (the sprout) will begin to form on the beans. Depending on the size of bean, this can take as little as a day or as much as 4 to 5 days.

Once the beans have sprouted, rinse and drain them one last time, let them sit out in a strainer for an hour or two to dry, seal them in a container, and store in the fridge. They last 2 to 4 days.

Method 2: Using a Sprouting Bag

A sprouting bag is a mold-resistant bag that is specifically designed for sprouting. We've listed a couple of suppliers in the "Resources" section on www.eatnakednow.com. Don't try to make one of these bags yourself, as they'll just get moldy. Most sprouting bags are made from hemp fiber with a small amount of linen. They're naturally resistant to mold and mildew, so you don't have to worry about your sprouts getting damaged by the bag.

Simply put the soaked and rinsed beans in the bag, and dip the whole bag in a bowl of filtered water. Let it soak for about 30 seconds, and then pull it out of the water and let the water drain out. We have a little hook right over our kitchen sink on which we hang our sprouting bag until it's stopped dripping.

Set the moist but not dripping sprouting bag in a bowl, and repeat the dip and drain procedure at least twice daily. You want the sprouts to remain moist but not sit in water for too long. Similar to mason jar sprouting, it's easiest to do this first thing in the morning and again at night.

When a small tail (the sprout) begins to form on the beans, you're good to go! Depending on the size of the bean, this can take as little as a day or as much as 4 to 5 days.

Once the beans have sprouted, rinse and drain them one last time, let them sit out in a strainer for an hour or two to dry, seal them in a container, and place in the fridge. They last 2 to 4 days.

Wash but Don't Sterilize Your Jars

Unlike in canning, whereby all equipment and jars must be sterilized in order to prevent harmful pathogens from infecting the food, you only need to wash your equipment and jars in warm soapy water when you culture food. Cultured foods are living foods, and a sterile environment isn't hospitable to the beneficial bacteria that are fundamental to the culturing process. Also, the lacto-fermentation process these good bacteria initiate reduces the pH of the food, making it an inhospitable environment for common pathogens. There's no guarantee, however, so use your instincts. If a cultured food smells "off" (a very different smell from sour—and your body will instinctively know), then don't take any chances: throw it out. We've been culturing foods for many years and haven't ever had any problems.

Culturing

Culturing, or "fermentation," is when naturally occurring bacteria convert sugars in a food into lactic acid or alcohol, both of which prevent spoilage. This was the earliest form of food preservation. Indeed, it's likely that culturing was the first true "cooking" technique—even before fire.

Unlike soaking and sprouting, which are really only used for grains, beans, nuts, and seeds, culturing is used for a wide variety of foods. We culture dairy into products such as yogurt, kefir, buttermilk, cheese, and cultured butter; we culture vegetables into sauerkraut and pickles; we culture fruits into chutneys and wine; we culture grains into sourdough bread, beer, and liquor. We can even culture fish and meats. Just about anything and everything can be cultured, and has been for centuries. Almost every society in the world has some form of cultured food integrated into its diet.

There are several ways of culturing foods—some health promoting, some not so much. When combined with water, all sugars and starches will ferment naturally if left to their own devices. Wild bacteria that exist in the air will convert the sugars to lactic acid, and eventually alcohol. You can also stimulate and to a certain degree control the culturing of foods by adding culture starters such as sea salt, whey, or yeast, or even commercially prepared culture powders, grains, or liquids. (Visit the "Resources" section on www.eatnakednow.com for a list of our favorites.)

The culturing process is very different from putrefaction or rotting, which happens to higher-protein-containing foods such as meats. When something rots, it is "off" and your nose will let you know it's not safe to eat. When something ferments, it has a naturally sour flavor and is a very healthful addition to your diet. In some cases this sour flavor is barely noticeable, for example in Cultured Salsa (page 68) or Cultured Butter (page 64), but in others such as the Cultured Vegetables recipes (pages 72 and 73) it's quite pronounced. How sour the dish is depends on how long you culture the food and the flavors in the recipe.

There are lots of reasons to include cultured foods in your diet. Much like soaking and sprouting, culturing enhances digestibility and neutralizes antinutrients. But that's just the beginning. As we addressed earlier, culturing is a natural method of food preservation. This means we can use culturing instead of nutrient-damaging processes such as the high heat used in canning, or the artificial preservatives added to so many processed foods.

Cultured foods are predigested and chock-full of enzymes. This means they digest easily and they enhance the digestion of anything that's eaten with them. Who needs to supplement with digestive enzymes when you can eat them as a delicious part of your meal?

The culturing process makes the nutrients in the food more available to your body and increases the nutrient content of the food itself. It also adds beneficial bacteria, called probiotics, to your food, which act as high-powered housekeepers to your intestines. Most nutrients are absorbed into your blood via the intestinal wall, which also happens to be home to approximately 80 percent of your immune system. This means that the probiotics in cultured foods improve nutrient absorption and strengthen your immune system. Superfoods indeed!

The processes for culturing foods differ depending on the food item. We've included several recipes for cultured foods including one for a starter for Whey (page 63); Cultured Butter (page 64); Yogurt (page 65); two different types of cultured vegetables—Sheree's Green Cultured Vegetables (page 72) and Spicy Sauerkraut (page 74)—and cultured versions of several common condiments such as Ketchup (page 66), Mustard (page 67), Mayonnaise (page 71), and two salsas—Cultured Salsa (page 68) and Spicy Salsa Verde (page 70).

Integrating Better Than Naked Foods into Your Diet

"Better than naked" food preparation isn't hard and doesn't take a lot of your time, but it does take planning and patience. And yes, these are two qualities you may not be accustomed to fostering in the kitchen. Most people are impatient when it comes to food.

Our advice to you is to start small and simply try out one or two recipes. For example, if you're going to have rice for dinner, put the uncooked rice in a bowl with water first thing in the morning before leaving for work. When you come home, it will have soaked all day and be ready to drain, rinse, and cook. Voilà! Your first "better than naked" cooking adventure.

To dip your toe into culturing foods, start with the Whey (page 63) culture starter. Much like the rice above, you can put yogurt out in a strainer in the morning before work, and when you get home, you'll have whey and homemade cream cheese. That was easy. Now you have the starter for most of the other cultured recipes. The whey stores in the fridge for up to several months, so you've got plenty of time to get organized and try another recipe.

Next, make it a habit to soak and then dehydrate or slow-roast any nut or seed (except the very small ones like flax and chia) as soon as you buy them. That way they'll be ready for you when you need them.

Once you get into the habit of having things soaking, sprouting, or culturing, you'll find that it's a new routine that's easily integrated into your lifestyle. At any given moment we'll usually have something soaking, sprouting, or culturing. It's just part of what we do. Take baby steps, and you'll find it's not that hard and doesn't take nearly as much time as you'd think.

PART 2

let's get cooking

How to Use These Recipes

Okay, it's time to roll up your sleeves, throw on that sexy apron, cue the tunes, and get cooking!

To help you figure out which recipes are right for the occasion, we've categorized each recipe into one of three time-sensitive brackets:

- **In a rush**, for those recipes that should take 10 minutes or less to prepare

- **Everyday**, for those recipes that should take between 10 and 30 minutes to prepare

- **Impress the neighbors**, for when time isn't a factor and you can pull out all the stops

A lot of these recipes use "better than naked" ingredients such as soaked nuts or a cultured salsa. These typically take some planning, so we encourage you to read through the recipes that you find particularly interesting; if they include some "better than naked" ingredients, consider preparing those ahead of time so you'll have them at the ready. If the recipe includes some "better than naked" ingredients or preparatory techniques, we've flagged that in the headline so you'll know at first glance.

We've crafted these recipes so that they build on each other, and we recommend starting with some basics or a couple of sauces and building up from there. The basics—plus sauces, dressings, and dips—are the kinds of foods most of us tend to buy premade, not really thinking about how processed they are when we automatically reach for them on store shelves. If you're ready to start building a naked kitchen, start here. We've found that if you have the basic condiments, sauces, and dressings already made, you're far more likely to use the homemade version. In the headline, we've identified those recipes that you make once and use lots, so you'll be able to find these easily while flipping through the book.

To further assist you, we've flagged each recipe as vegan, vegetarian, pescatarian, or omnivore. For many of the omnivore and pescatarian recipes, we've included vegetarian options. For the purposes of this book, recipes that include bee pollen and honey are considered vegan.

In keeping with our naked philosophy, we've included soy only in its fermented forms. We've also kept 100 percent of our recipes gluten-free, since gluten is a problem for so many people and it's really not a necessary ingredient. For all ingredients, we recommend finding the most naked versions you can, within reason.

You may notice we have some canned products listed in some of the recipes. While we would love to recommend that you buy fresh tomatoes and peel, seed, and cook them yourself, we realize that just doesn't fit into most people's schedules. Also, good fresh, local tomatoes aren't available year-round. Use your discretion when you see any mention of something canned. If you have the time to make the item from scratch (like beans, tomatoes, or coconut milk), then by all means do so. Our goal is to help you make as many of your meals at home as possible. If that means using canned beans or canned tomatoes, then don't sweat it. Just look for canned products with as little sodium as possible, and without any of those unpronounceable ingredients.

And remember: these recipes are a starting point. Try them as they are and then feel free to experiment. Swap out ingredients, mix it up, try sauces with any steamed or sautéed veggies. There are so many things you can do. Have fun with it, and certainly don't take any of it too seriously.

Without further ado, let's get cooking!

5
Basics

The recipes in this section are foundational recipes that are used in many of the other recipes throughout this book. With only a few exceptions, they are of the "Make it once, use it lots" variety. In other words, you won't be making them on a daily basis. We recommend making one or two of these on a weekend (which ones you pick will depend on what you're planning for the week) so you have them throughout the rest of your week.

FLAX EGG

In a rush •• Vegan •• Raw •• Make it once, use it lots

If you're baking and a recipe calls for an egg but you don't eat them for whatever reason, here's a solution: the flax egg. When ground up and combined with water, flax yields a similar consistency and effect as the egg. Substitute two tablespoons of flax egg for every egg in the recipe.

Note that this isn't an egg substitute for recipes across the board. It's just for baking. (You're not going to have a flax egg omelet for breakfast!)

Makes 1 cup

¼ cup flaxseeds

Put flax seeds in a food processor and grind. With the food processor still running, slowly drizzle in ¾ cup water. Let the food processor continue to run until the mixture has thickened. You'll notice that the mixture starts to congeal slightly and gets a little foamy. This means it's ready.

Store in a glass jar in the refrigerator for up to 1 week.

Note: If you're storing the flax eggs, the flax continues to absorb the liquid and will become paste-like. You may need to add a little filtered water to the mix prior to using it.

NUT CRUST

In a rush •• Vegetarian, with vegan option •• Better than naked •• Make it once, use it lots

Here's another example of a gluten-free and delicious alternative to a comfort-food favorite. Using a nut crust simulates that "fried chicken" feeling without the deep-frying. Nut crusts are a great way to get kids to eat their meat, because you add great flavor and a crunchy texture to your dinner without the fillers and gluten that you find in breaded products. We use it for Nut-Crusted Pesto Chicken (page 187), but you can also use it on fish, pork, lamb, or eggplant.

For a vegan version of this crust, omit the Parmesan.

Makes 2½ cups

- 1 cup almonds, ideally presoaked and dehydrated or slow-roasted
- 1 cup pumpkin seeds or pepitas, ideally presoaked and dehydrated or slow-roasted
- ½ cup fresh parsley
- 1 tablespoon granulated garlic
- 1 teaspoon sea salt
- 1 teaspoon paprika
- ½ teaspoon freshly ground pepper
- 1 tablespoon grated Parmesan (optional)

Combine all ingredients in a food processor and pulse several times until nuts are chopped. Store in the fridge in a sealed container until ready to use.

ALMOND MILK

In a rush •• Vegan •• Better than naked •• Make it once, use it lots

Almond milk is another great substitute for cow's or goat's milk. As with many nondairy milks, the problem with buying it commercially is that it often has additives to emulsify and preserve it. Making your own gives you total control over the ingredients, and, as a nice bonus, the flavor is unparalleled—it's lighter, fresher, and much more delicious. It's a great addition to smoothies, dressings, and curry sauces, or you can use it anytime you'd use milk.

Store almond milk in the refrigerator. It keeps for about 1 week. If the almond meal and water separate after sitting, just give it a good shake before you use it.

Makes 2½ cups

2 cups raw almonds, soaked for at least 8 hours

1 teaspoon vanilla extract

2 pitted dates

Using a dishtowel, squeeze each soaked almond to remove the skin. Combine the peeled almonds with the vanilla, the dates, and 3 cups filtered water in a high-powered blender. Purée until smooth.

Line a sieve with some cheesecloth and strain the almond milk to get rid of any bits. Store in the refrigerator in a glass jar and use as you would milk.

You can use the leftover almond bits in a smoothie or in cookies.

COCONUT MILK

In a rush •• Vegan •• Raw •• Make it once, use it lots

Coconut milk is a great substitute for dairy and is used in several of our recipes. As with many nondairy milks, the problem with buying it commercially is that it often has additives to emulsify and preserve it. Making your own gives you total control over the ingredients and, as a nice bonus, the flavor is unparalleled—it's lighter, fresher, and much more delicious. It's a great addition to smoothies, dressings, curry sauces, or anything else that calls for cow's milk.

Store coconut milk in the refrigerator. It keeps for about 1 week. You'll notice the water and meat separate after it sits. Just give it a good shake before you use it and you're good to go.

Makes approximately 2 cups

1 young green coconut

Open the coconut (visit www.eatnakednow.com/videos for a video on how to easily open a coconut) and pour the water from the coconut into a blender. Following the circumference of the shell, pressing firmly with a spoon, strip the coconut meat away from the shell. You may still get slivers of shell stuck to the coconut meat. Just pull them off with your fingers. Add coconut meat to blender and pulverize until well mixed. Store in a glass container in the fridge until ready to use. Stores for up to 1 week. Shake well before using.

Notes: If the coconut water is a little pink, the coconut is not yet ripe, and you won't be able to use the meat. You can drink the water safely, but you won't be able to make coconut milk. If the coconut water is gray or really cloudy, it has gone rancid, and you'll have to throw the whole thing out. Unfortunately, there's no easy and reliable way to tell whether a coconut is ripe before you open it. We recommend that you buy more than one at a time in case you get a bad coconut, or have canned coconut milk on hand if it's needed in a recipe.

LENTILS

Everyday •• Vegan, with vegetarian, pescatarian, and omnivore options •• Make it once, use it lots

Preparing your own beans takes a little time but saves you money and the extra sodium you'll often find in canned beans. Lentils are among the easiest to prepare, because they don't require soaking in advance of cooking. We've put them in the "everyday" category, because they do take about 30 minutes to cook. Most of that time is unattended, however, so they can be cooking while you're doing other things.

For the vegan version of this recipe use water to cook the lentils; for the vegetarian version, use Kitchen Scraps Veggie Stock; for a pescatarian version, use either Dashi or Fish Stock; and for an omnivore version, use Beef Bone Broth.

Makes 3 cups

> **4 cups water or stock such as Kitchen Scraps Veggie Stock (page 50), Dashi (page 59), Fish Stock (page 48), or Beef Bone Broth (page 49)**
>
> **2 cups dried lentils (green, red, or French)**
>
> **1 tablespoon coriander seeds**
>
> **2 bay leaves**
>
> **1 teaspoon dried fennel seeds**

Put the water or stock, lentils, coriander, bay leaves, and fennel in a large saucepan. Cover and bring to a boil on high heat. Turn heat down to low, still covered, and let simmer for approximately 30 minutes. Check the lentils after 20 minutes for desired consistency. Green lentils will get very soft; French lentils are best al dente or firmer; red lentils soften quickly and purée well.

Drain lentils and either use immediately, or store in the refrigerator for up to 4 days.

BROWN RICE FRY BATTER

Everyday •• Vegan

This is a light, gluten-free, and very easy alternative to your normal frying batter. We use it for our Light and Crispy Chicken Bites (page 183), but you can also use it on vegetables, fish, or any kind of meat.

Makes 1 cup

>   ½ cup brown rice flour
>
>   ¼ cup arrowroot
>
>   1 teaspoon baking soda
>
>   ½ teaspoon sea salt
>
>   ¼ to ½ cup very cold still or carbonated water

Combine the dry ingredients in a medium-sized bowl and mix well. Add the water and stir to make batter. You don't want the batter to be too thick. Add more water if necessary.

Use the batter quickly. If it sits for too long, you may need to add more liquid.

Tip: Buy your arrowroot in large quantities. The small spice containers you typically find it in are too small and expensive. See the resource page on www.eatnakednow. com for places to buy it.

FISH STOCK

Everyday •• Pescatarian •• Make it once, use it lots

Fish stock makes an excellent base for any Asian-style soup. The base for the soup is fish bones and scraps. To find fish bones, ask your fishmonger to save some for you since most fish now come already filleted with the bones removed. We specify below to use a pot with a heavy bottom. This is important for stock because you cook it for such a long time that it could burn with a thin-bottomed pot. Try it in the No-Frills Miso Soup (page 157) or Hearty Miso Soup (page 162).

This recipe includes some kombu seaweed for its rich mineral content. You can find it at your local Asian market or health food store.

Although this recipe cooks for more than 8 to 12 hours, we've included it in the "everyday" category, because the bulk of this time is unattended, and your time is used only minimally at the beginning and end of the process.

Makes 4 to 6 cups

> 10 ounces fish bones, head, skin, and scraps
>
> 1 piece (2 to 4 inches) kombu seaweed
>
> ½ cup coarsely chopped fresh ginger
>
> 3 stalks celery, coarsely chopped, or the equivalent in discarded leafy tops (approximately 1½ cups)
>
> 1 unpeeled onion, quartered
>
> 1 jalapeño pepper, halved (optional: seed if you're worried about stock being too spicy)
>
> 1 tablespoon apple cider vinegar

Combine all ingredients with 10 cups filtered water in a heavy-bottomed 8-quart pot. Cover and bring to a boil. When water is boiling, remove lid, turn heat to lowest setting possible, and let simmer for 8 to 12 hours, until stock has been reduced by approximately half.

Skim any foam off the top, strain, and either use immediately as a base for soup, or store in the refrigerator after it has cooled and use within 1 week. To store it for longer than 1 week, let it cool and then store it in freezer bags in the freezer.

BEEF BONE BROTH

Everyday •• Omnivore •• Make it once, use it lots

Bone broth is one of the most deeply nourishing of the traditional foods, and it can be used as the basis for many different soups and sauces. It is typically made using bones and those cuts of meat that are too tough to eat. Ask your butcher or local farmer for bone and meat scraps you can use for broth. We use it as a base for Zesty Pulled Beef (page 194), Quinoa (page 54), and Stephanie's Family Rice (page 55).

Although this recipe cooks for more than 8 to 12 hours, we've included it in the "everyday" category, because the bulk of this time is unattended, and your time is used only minimally at the beginning and end of the process.

Makes 8 cups

> **4 pounds knuckle bones (or you can use beef marrow, neck bones, or meaty rib bones, or a combination of these)**
>
> **4 carrots, coarsely chopped**
>
> **2 celery stalks, coarsely chopped**
>
> **1 onion, peeled and coarsely chopped**
>
> **4 garlic cloves, halved**
>
> **¼ green apple, seeded**
>
> **½ bunch fresh parsley (stems and all)**
>
> **2 bay leaves**
>
> **1 tablespoon peppercorns**
>
> **2 tablespoons white vinegar**

Combine all ingredients with 14 cups filtered water in a heavy-bottomed 8-quart pot. Cover and bring to a boil. When water is boiling, remove lid, turn heat to lowest setting possible, and let simmer for 8 to 12 hours, until stock has been reduced by approximately half.

Skim any foam off the top, strain, and either use immediately as a base for soup or store in the refrigerator after it has cooled and use within 1 week. To store it for longer than 1 week, let it cool and then store it in freezer bags in the freezer.

KITCHEN SCRAPS VEGGIE STOCK

Everyday •• Vegetarian •• Make it once, use it lots

This is an excellent way to make use of all those veggie scraps that are created as you're making other dishes. Use carrot ends (not the tops—carrot greens are very bitter), celery fronds, onion ends, and so on. This is a particularly good stock to make on a day when you're doing a bunch of food prep all at once, because you'll have more scraps to work with.

It's important to include the eggshells, as these add minerals you're missing without having the bones you'd normally be using for stock. The vinegar helps to draw out the minerals from the eggshells, so it's an important ingredient too.

Although this recipe cooks for more than 8 to 12 hours, we've included it in the "everyday" category, because the bulk of this time is unattended, and your time is used only minimally at the beginning and end of the process.

Makes 4 to 6 cups

Shells from 4 to 6 eggs

4 to 8 cups of veggie scraps—they don't even need to be chopped, they just need to be clean; try celery, garlic, onion, peppers, carrots (but not carrot greens), parsnips, any kind of squash, zucchini, or green beans

1 teaspoon white vinegar

Combine all ingredients in a heavy-bottomed 8-quart pot. Add 10 cups filtered water. Cover and bring to a boil. When water is boiling, remove lid, turn the heat to lowest setting possible, and let simmer for 8 to 12 hours, until stock has been reduced.

Skim any foam off the top, strain, and either use immediately as a base for soup or store in the refrigerator after it has cooled and use within 1 week. To store it for longer than 1 week, let it cool and then store it in freezer bags in the freezer.

RAW COCONUT BUTTER

Everyday •• Vegan •• Raw •• Make it once, use it lots

Raw coconut butter is a great substitute for oversweetened spreads. Use it anywhere you'd use a nut butter. We even treat it like yogurt or cottage cheese, adding fruit for a refreshing snack. It's allergen-free, a great source of lauric acid (an antimicrobial), and an excellent source of quick energy (the medium-chain fatty acids in coconut are easily converted into fuel by your body).

Makes 1 generous cup

3 to 4 cups shredded unsweetened raw coconut

1 teaspoon cinnamon

½ teaspoon vanilla extract

Using a food processor, blend coconut for 8 to 10 minutes or until it starts to form a smooth paste. Stop the food processor occasionally and scrape down the sides with a flexible spatula to ensure it's all blending together. At first it will appear as though nothing's happening, but the consistency will change with time and patience.

Add cinnamon and vanilla, and continue blending until smooth. It will have the consistency of a creamy nut butter.

Store in a mason jar in a cool cupboard. Do not store in the fridge—the cold will harden the butter and make it extremely difficult to work with. The oil may separate over time. Just mix it well before using.

Note: Do not use low-fat, sweetened, or processed coconut. The recipe works only with full-fat, unprocessed shredded coconut.

COCONUT RICE

Everyday •• Vegan, with vegetarian and pescatarian options •• Better than naked •• Make it once, use it lots

This is an easy way to take your usual brown rice and turn it into a delicious, flavorful side. It makes use of a "better than naked" cooking technique by having you presoak the rice for several hours. As with many "better than naked" recipes, this adds time to the preparation but requires almost no additional work, just a little planning.

For the vegan version of this recipe use water to cook the rice; for the vegetarian version, use Kitchen Scraps Veggie Stock; and for a pescatarian version, use either Dashi or Fish Stock.

Makes 4 servings

> 1 cup brown basmati rice
>
> 1 cup water, Kitchen Scraps Veggie Stock (page 50), Dashi (page 59), or Fish Stock (page 48)
>
> ½ cup canned or homemade Coconut Milk (page 41)
>
> 1 teaspoon unrefined coconut oil
>
> 1 (1-inch) piece ginger root, peeled (optional)
>
> Pinch sea salt
>
> 2 tablespoons minced cilantro (optional)

Put basmati rice in a large bowl and cover with filtered water. Soak for 8 to 24 hours. Drain rice and rinse well.

In a large saucepan with lid on, bring the water or broth and coconut milk to a boil. Add rice, coconut oil, ginger, and sea salt. Cover and bring back to a boil, then reduce heat to low and let simmer, still covered, for 15 to 20 minutes, until all water has been absorbed.

Remove the ginger and serve with cilantro sprinkled over top.

VANILLA HEMP MILK

Everyday •• Vegan •• Better than naked •• Make it once, use it lots

If you're sensitive to dairy or aren't able to find a quality source of milk, hemp milk is an excellent alternative. Soy milk, once so favored by health enthusiasts, is highly processed and uses unfermented soy beans, making it extremely taxing on your digestive system. Hemp milk is delicious and easy to make. Use it just as you would any other flavored milk.

As with many nondairy milks, the problem with buying it commercially is that it often has additives to emulsify and preserve it. Making your own gives you total control over the ingredients. Store hemp milk in the refrigerator. It keeps for about 1 week.

While this recipe includes 24 hours of soaking time, we've put it in the "everyday" category because your attention isn't required while it's soaking.

Makes 2½ cups

1 cup organic hemp seeds

2 teaspoons vanilla extract

2 pitted dates

Put hemp seeds in a medium bowl and cover generously with filtered water. Let soak at room temperature for 24 hours. Drain and rinse well. This will yield approximately 1½ cups of soaked seeds.

Combine the seeds, the vanilla, the dates, and 3 cups filtered water in a high-powered blender. Purée until well mixed. Line a sieve with cheesecloth and set it on top of a bowl. Pour the milk through to filter out any bits. Store it in the refrigerator for up to 1 week. You'll have to give it a shake before using it (without fancy emulsifiers, the water and hemp will separate when it sits).

QUINOA

Everyday •• Vegan, with vegetarian, pescatarian, and omnivore options •• Better than naked •• Make it once, use it lots

Quinoa is one of those gluten-free grains that's a favorite of the health-food community. It's higher in protein than most other grains, making it a particularly good grain for vegetarians. We use it in the Quinoa Vegetable Sushi (page 200) and Quinoa Tabouleh (page 117), but it also works well as a side with just about any vegetable or protein dish.

This recipe makes use of a "better than naked" cooking technique by having you presoak the quinoa for several hours. As with many "better than naked" recipes, this adds prep time but requires almost no additional work, just a little planning. For this reason, we've kept it in the "everyday" category.

For the vegan version of this recipe, use water to cook the quinoa; for the vegetarian version, use Kitchen Scraps Veggie Stock; for a pescatarian version, use either Dashi or Fish Stock; and for an omnivore version, use Beef Bone Broth.

Makes 2½ cups

> **1 cup quinoa (we use a combination of red and white quinoa)**
>
> **1½ cups filtered water or Kitchen Scraps Veggie Stock (page 50), Dashi (page 59), Fish Stock (page 48), or Beef Bone Broth (page 49)**

Put quinoa in a large bowl and cover generously with plain filtered water. Make sure there's 1 inch of water above the top of the grains. Let sit at room temperature for 1 to 4 hours. Drain and rinse the quinoa well.

Bring the water, stock, or broth to a boil in a medium saucepan with the lid on. When boiling, add the soaked and rinsed grains, cover the pot, and bring back to a boil. When boiling, with lid still on, turn down heat to low and let cook for 15 to 20 minutes, until all water has been absorbed.

If serving hot, use immediately. If serving cold, spread the cooked quinoa out on an oven tray and leave at room temperature to cool. (Spreading it out in this way speeds up the cooling process.)

Tip: To make your quinoa ultralight and fluffy, after it has soaked and you've drained and rinsed it, and while you're waiting for the water, stock, or broth to boil, spread the quinoa out on a dry skillet, and heat it over low heat, stirring often, until the moisture has evaporated. Don't go too far from the stove while you're doing this or you'll burn it. Add it to the boiling water as per the usual recipe, and you're sailing.

STEPHANIE'S FAMILY RICE

Impress the neighbors •• Omnivore, with vegetarian option •• Better than naked •• Make it once, use it lots

This rice dish is one our friend Stephanie makes in great quantity for her family on a weekly basis. Using a combination of rices, soaking them for maximum nutrient availability, cooking them in broth rather than water, and adding a pat of butter at the end makes this a nutrient-dense side to complement any meal. We like to double or even triple the recipe, so that we make it once and have it for use in a variety of ways throughout the week. Oh, and kids love it.

If you're not able to find the specific rices and seeds we specify below, look for a whole-grain rice blend and use 1½ cups of it. Just make sure the only ingredients are the rices and seeds, no extra flavorings or additives.

This recipe makes use of a "better than naked" cooking technique by having you presoak the rice for several hours. As with many "better than naked" recipes, this adds prep time but requires almost no additional work, just a little planning.

For a vegetarian version of this recipe, use Kitchen Scraps Veggie Stock instead of Beef Bone Broth.

Makes 6 servings

> **1 cup long-grain brown rice**
>
> **¼ cup wild rice**
>
> **¼ cup daikon radish seeds**
>
> **2½ cups Beef Bone Broth (page 49) or Kitchen Scraps Veggie Stock (page 50)**
>
> **2 tablespoons butter (ideally Cultured Butter, page 64)**
>
> **1 teaspoon red pepper flakes**
>
> **½ teaspoon sea salt**

Put brown rice, wild rice, and radish seeds in a large bowl and cover generously with filtered water. Make sure there's an inch of water above the top of the grains. Let sit at room temperature for 8 to 24 hours. Drain and rinse well.

Bring the broth or stock to a boil in a medium saucepan with the lid on. When boiling, add the soaked and rinsed grains, cover the pot, and bring back to a boil. Once boiling, with lid still on, turn down heat to low and let cook for 35 to 45 minutes, until all water has been absorbed.

Remove rice from heat. Add butter, broken into little chunks, over the top of the rice. Put lid back on the pot, and let the butter melt from the residual heat. Transfer the rice to a bowl and sprinkle with red pepper flakes and sea salt.

GHEE

Impress the neighbors •• Vegetarian •• Make it once, use it lots

Ghee, or clarified butter, is an excellent option for baking and high-temperature cooking because the milk proteins—those little white bits that burn so easily when you cook with butter—have been removed. Ghee is essentially the oil found in butter. It's used often in Indian cuisine, and we use it regularly for anything that's cooked at a higher temperature. Ghee is also safe for many people with a dairy sensitivity, since the protein, which is what most folks are sensitive to, has been cooked out.

Makes 1½ to 1¾ cups

2 cups organic, unsalted butter, ideally from pasture-fed cows

Put butter in a small saucepan over medium-low heat. Butter will melt and then simmer. It will start to bubble gently with a kind of popping sound. Make sure it doesn't actually boil. You'll notice that white milk solids will separate from the butter oil and eventually settle to the bottom of the saucepan. This takes approximately 30 minutes. When all of the milk solids have settled to the bottom, the ghee is ready. Sometimes a few stubborn solids stay at the top—just skim these off.

Using a fine strainer, pour the oil into a glass jar. The strainer will catch any bits of milk solid still in the oil. Leave uncovered at room temperature to cool. Then cover it with a lid and store it in a cool, dark cupboard. Ghee keeps for several months, and you don't need to refrigerate it.

CRISPY SHIITAKE FAUX BACON

Impress the neighbors •• Vegan •• Make it once use it lots

Even the most adamant non–mushroom eater will love these shiitakes. They're crispy, a little zesty, and so yummy. They taste surprisingly like bacon but are totally vegan. Use them in salads, miso soup, rice, sautés…anything in which you want the flavor and texture of bacon, without the bacon itself. We use them in our Caesar Salad (page 123) and Asian Fusion Salad (page 116).

Makes 1 cup

2 tablespoons unrefined coconut oil

8 to 10 large shiitake mushrooms, cut lengthwise into ¼-inch-thick slices (approximately 4 cups)

2 tablespoons gluten-free tamari soy sauce

Preheat oven to 395°F. If your kitchen is a little cool and the coconut oil is solid, put coconut oil in a heat-resistant bowl in the oven to let it melt while oven is preheating.

When coconut oil has melted, remove from the oven and mix well with the mushrooms. You may want to use your clean hands to work the oil into the mushrooms fully. Add the tamari, and continue mixing until well coated.

Spread mushrooms out on an oven tray and bake for 12 to 15 minutes. Flip the mushrooms with a stainless steel spatula, and keep baking for another 12 to 15 minutes, until nice and crispy.

BREADLESS STUFFING

Impress the neighbors •• Vegetarian, with vegan option •• Better than naked

Unlike most stuffing, this uses lentils as its base rather than breadcrumbs. This neatly solves the main problem with stuffing for those who are gluten-intolerant or are looking to reduce the starchy carbs from their diet. It does take a little work, hence we put it in the "impress the neighbors" category, but usually we're making stuffing for a special occasion anyhow. It's flavorful and a great alternative to your usual fare.

For a vegan option, substitute coconut oil for the ghee or butter.

Makes 4 to 5 cups

> 2 tablespoons ghee, butter, or unrefined coconut oil
>
> ½ head cauliflower
>
> 1 onion, diced (approximately 1 cup)
>
> 2 cloves garlic, peeled
>
> 2 celery stalks, diced (approximately 1 cup)
>
> 2 carrots, diced (approximately 1 cup)
>
> 1 teaspoon sea salt
>
> ½ teaspoon freshly ground pepper
>
> ¼ teaspoon paprika
>
> 1 cup green lentils
>
> 1 bay leaf
>
> 1 teaspoon thyme
>
> ½ cup chopped raw pecans (ideally presoaked and dehydrated or slow-roasted)
>
> ½ cup unsweetened dried fruit (cherries, cranberries, apricots, or a combination thereof)

Preheat oven to 375°F. If your kitchen is cool and the ghee is solid, put it in the oven in a heat-resistant mixing bowl to melt while the oven is heating.

Coarsely chop the cauliflower and put it in a food processor. Pulse several times to break down the cauliflower into fine pieces (only pulse several times, as you still want some larger chunks).

In a mixing bowl, toss cauliflower, onion, garlic cloves, celery, and carrots with ghee, sea salt, pepper, and paprika. Coat well with the oil. Spread mixture out on an oven tray, and roast for 15 to 20 minutes, until cooked through and slightly browned.

While cauliflower is roasting, cook the lentils: In a medium saucepan, combine lentils, bay leaf, and 2 cups filtered water. Cover and bring to a boil. Reduce heat and simmer, still covered, for 30 to 45 minutes, until lentils are cooked through. If water remains, drain it. Remove bay leaf and discard. Lentils should still hold their shape and not be mushy.

In a large mixing bowl, mix the veggies, thyme, pecans, and dried fruit. Use as you would normal stuffing.

DASHI

Everyday •• Pescatarian •• Make it once, use it lots

Dashi is a very speedy fish broth, using bonito flakes rather than bones. Bonito flakes are made from mackerel that's been steamed, dried, and shaved into flakes. You can find them at your local Asian market or health food store. They can be used cold as a seasoning or boiled into a soup like we're doing here. This makes an excellent and nutrient-rich base for Miso Soup (page 57 for a speedy version or page 162 for a heartier version).

Makes 3½ cups

1 (4-inch) piece kombu seaweed

½ cup bonito flakes

In a large saucepan, bring 4 cups filtered water to a boil with the piece of kombu. Add bonito flakes, turn off heat, and let soak for 10 minutes.

Strain stock and either use immediately or let cool and store in the fridge.

GLUTEN-FREE PIZZA DOUGH

Impress the neighbors •• Vegan •• Better than naked

We're always striving to show that just because something doesn't have gluten doesn't mean it's not tasty. This recipe shows that gluten-free baking isn't only easy, it's delicious too.

The whole point of kneading most dough is to work the gluten to make it malleable. In this case there's no gluten to work, which means no kneading. Use this dough for your favorite pizza. Some of our favorites are Salami Pizza (page 186), Mediterranean Veggie Pizza (page 185), and Barbeque-Inspired Chicken Pizza (page 184).

This recipe uses almonds or almond meal. You can make your own "better than naked" almond meal from presoaked and dehydrated or slow-roasted almonds. To make 1 cup of almond meal, simply put a generous cup of almonds into your food processor and process until it achieves a flour-like consistency. It takes only a minute or two.

Makes dough for 2 medium or 1 large pizza

- 1 cup raw almonds (ideally presoaked and dehydrated or slow-roasted) or almond meal
- ½ cup plus 2 tablespoons sorghum flour
- ½ cup arrowroot
- 1 packet active dry yeast (2 teaspoons)
- 1 teaspoon sea salt
- 1 tablespoon plus 1 teaspoon extra-virgin olive oil
- ½ teaspoon raw honey

If using raw almonds, put almonds into food processor and run until they've been finely ground into almond meal. If using preground almond meal, put it in the food processor and proceed to the next step.

Switch blades on the food processor to the plastic dough blade. Add the sorghum flour, arrowroot, yeast, and salt into the food processor. Pulse several times to combine the dry ingredients. With the processor running, slowly pour in ½ cup lukewarm water, then add 1 tablespoon of olive oil and the honey. Let blend until the dough begins to clump. Using a rubber spatula, scrape down the sides of the processor, and process again. Continue scraping and processing until the dough has formed into a ball in the processor. Note: it's important to use a rubber spatula, not a metal spatula, as the metal has a damaging effect on the yeast.

Using a spatula, turn dough out of the food processor and roll it into a ball. Using the remaining olive oil, coat a medium mixing bowl. Put the dough in the bowl, turning it to coat all sides with the oil. Cover the bowl with a clean towel and leave it in a warm spot in your kitchen, undisturbed, for an hour and a half. Unlike dough containing gluten, this dough will rise only a very little bit.

Use immediately or store in the refrigerator tightly wrapped in plastic to keep moist. We sometimes make big batches of this dough and then divide it into individual portions, wrapped tightly in plastic and then stored in zip-top bags in the freezer for later use.

6
Better Than Naked

L ike many of the recipes in the "Basics" chapter, these recipes are good to make once, and use many times. Adding a "better than naked" product to your meals has never been easier. We've included a few different options to try in this chapter, from cultured condiments and cultured vegetables to cultured dairy products.

Cultured products are not new. They've been around for more than a thousand years— the industrial, sugar-laden condiments like modern ketchup have been around only since the early 1900s. Condiments of today are a mere shadow of the nutritional powerhouses of the past. Traditionally, salsas, ketchups, and relishes were used not only to add flavor and texture to dishes, but also to act as digestive aids. They are filled with beneficial bacteria and enzymes from the natural culturing process that preserves the food and helps you digest it. With the advent of industrial food production, these traditional food-preservation techniques have been long forgotten and replaced with artificial preservatives or high-pressure and high-heat processing techniques that damage the food. The time has come to bring back the old customs and reinvigorate our diets with preventative foods.

Don't let the culturing process scare you from trying these recipes. There are many ways of culturing (see chapter 4 for "better than naked" preparation techniques). Some of the recipes such as cultured vegetables will be time consuming the first time, but the more you make them the faster you'll get. We recommend taking one day during the weekend to make a few of the "better than naked" recipes. They will last several months in your fridge, and the health benefits are well worth the time investment. We like to make sure there's always some Whey (page 63) in the fridge, since it's used in so many recipes, as well as at least one jar of cultured veggies, since they add that extra digestive boost to everything. So get your caveperson on and get culturing!

WHEY AND CULTURED CREAM CHEESE

In a rush •• Vegetarian •• Better than naked •• Make it once, use it lots

Whey is used as a culture starter in many of our recipes. If you prefer, you can buy non-dairy culture starters (see the resource section of www.eatnakednow.com for our favorites). But if dairy is fine, then making whey is easy to do in your own kitchen with just one very common ingredient: yogurt. We use the by-product of making whey—homemade cream cheese—in our Mediterranean Party Dip (page 141).

Even though to get the end result takes 8 to 10 hours for this recipe, we've put it in the "in a rush" category because it takes almost none of your time, just the time for gravity to do its thing and the whey to drip through. The amount of whey and cream cheese you make depends on how big a container of yogurt you start with and the thickness of the yogurt. If you start with 1 cup of yogurt you'll typically get about ½ cup whey and ½ cup cream cheese. Don't use Greek-style yogurt when making whey, since it has already been strained to make it so thick and will produce very little whey.

1 container (any size) organic plain yogurt with live active cultures

Line a sieve with a clean, fine-weave dishtowel or two to three layers of cheesecloth, and set

it on top of a clean bowl. Pour the yogurt into the towel-lined sieve, which will allow the clear, yellowish liquid (the whey) to drip through the sieve into the bowl. This takes between 8 and 10 hours. We often let it sit out overnight.

When all the whey has dripped into the bowl, you're left with what is essentially home-made cream cheese in the sieve. You can use it as you would cream cheese, or add some sea salt and flavorings to it such as sun-dried tomatoes, olives, spinach, or fresh herbs. See the Mediterranean Party Dip recipe for some ideas.

Store the whey in a glass jar in the refrigerator. It keeps for months.

CULTURED BUTTER AND BUTTERMILK

In a rush •• Vegetarian •• Better than naked •• Make it once, use it lots

Making your own butter sounds exotic but is surprisingly easy. All that's needed is a pint of raw cream, a food processor, and a few minutes of your time. The flavor is out of this world, and assuming you're getting high-quality cream from healthy, grass-fed cows (which is a must if you're getting raw cream), then the nutritional value of this butter is as high as it gets.

Cultured butter is butter that's made from cream that has been slightly cultured. The result is a more nutritionally dense butter with a very subtle sour flavor. It's delicious.

Even though to get the end result takes 8 hours for this recipe, we've put it in the "in a rush" category because it takes almost none of your time.

Makes approximately 1 cup butter and 1 cup buttermilk

2 cups raw cream (you can also use organic crème fraîche if you don't have access to raw cream)

¼ teaspoon sea salt (optional)

Let cream sit at room temperature for 8 hours to sour slightly. If you're using crème fraîche, you can skip this step, as it is already soured. Pour the cream into a food processor with a steel blade and process until butter forms. It takes very little time—3 to 4 minutes—and you'll hear a noticeable change in the sound of the processor when the butter has formed. You'll notice that liquid has separated from the butter; this is the buttermilk.

Using a spatula, press the clumps of butter together and against the side of the food processor to squeeze out extra buttermilk. Scoop out the butter and put it into a separate bowl, pressing down on it with your spatula to squeeze out more of the buttermilk. Repeat until no more buttermilk comes out.

Pour the buttermilk left in the food processor and from the bowl into a mason jar, and store in the fridge for up to a month. Use it for Carrot Cake (page 242), Chocolate Cupcakes (page 244), or Apple Pancakes (page 92).

Add the salt to the butter and stir to blend. Store in the fridge in a sealed container.

YOGURT

Everyday •• Vegetarian •• Better than naked •• Make it once, use it lots

Making your own yogurt is not only surprisingly easy, it's also better for your health because you can control the quality of the ingredients. Yogurt made in your kitchen begins with few tablespoons of store-bought yogurt, so it's very important to start with a very good quality yogurt. Check that the yogurt you're using has active bacterial cultures in it. These are the cultures that will make your new batch of yogurt, so they're crucial.

Make sure the yogurt you're using as a starter is at room temperature. This allows the active cultures in the yogurt to wake up. They go dormant when refrigerated.

As with some of the other recipes in this chapter, it takes 8 to 10 hours for the yogurt to culture. We've put it in the "everyday" category, as your time is required only at the beginning of this process.

Makes 4 cups

3½ cups raw or pasteurized organic milk

2 heaping tablespoons room-temperature organic plain yogurt with active bacterial cultures (a commercial variety is fine) or from a previous batch of homemade yogurt

In a medium saucepan, heat the milk to 180°F (use a food thermometer to gauge the temperature of the milk). Pour warmed milk into large bowl, and allow to cool to 110°F. Add the yogurt, and stir to mix. Pour into a quart-size mason jar, cover, and keep warm overnight (ideally between 95°F and 110°F). You can put it in a food dehydrator set to 110°F, a gas oven with a pilot light on, or an oven heated to its lowest setting (150°F) and then turned off, with door closed, overnight. It takes 8 to 10 hours.

In the morning, put the yogurt in the fridge. It will be slightly runnier than commercial varieties, but is still delicious. To thicken it, you can drain it using a fine sieve and cheesecloth, but the amount of yogurt will be lessened significantly. Add your own fresh or frozen fruit to make a flavored yogurt without the additional sugar you'd find in commercial yogurt.

KETCHUP

Everyday •• Vegetarian, with vegan option •• Better than naked •• Make it once, use it lots

Ketchup is a great example of a healthful condiment turned sugar-laden processed food product. Like many condiments, ketchup was traditionally made using fermentation to preserve it, which had the handy side effect of adding probiotics and enzymes that aid digestion. This recipe returns us to these traditional methods and creates delicious ketchup that is actually good for you.

As with other recipes in this chapter, it takes 2 days for the ketchup to culture. We've put it in the "everyday" category, as your time is required only at the beginning of this process.

For the vegan version of this recipe, use nondairy culture starter powder instead of Whey. We've put a list of our favorite brands in the "Resources" section on www.eatnakednow.com.

Makes 3 cups

    1 small onion, coarsely chopped

    ½ teaspoon ground cumin

    ¼ teaspoon ground clove

    ½ teaspoon powdered mustard

    ½ teaspoon sea salt

    1 (28-ounce) can diced tomatoes, drained

    1 (6-ounce) can tomato paste

    3 tablespoons unsulphured blackstrap molasses

    2 tablespoons apple cider vinegar

    ¼ cup Whey (page 63) or 1 packet nondairy culture starter powder

Heat a medium skillet over medium heat until hot. Add chopped onion, ½ cup water, the cumin, clove, powdered mustard, and sea salt, and sauté for 2 to 4 minutes, until translucent. The water will evaporate almost completely. Remove from heat and add to a blender along with remaining ingredients. Blend until smooth.

Pour ketchup into mason jars, making sure to leave an inch between the top of the ketchup and the top of the jar. Cover with lid and let stand at room temperature for 2 days to culture. Store in the fridge. Will keep for up to several months.

MUSTARD

Everyday •• Vegetarian, with vegan option •• Better than naked •• Make it once, use it lots

Want to keep unnecessary additives, sugar, and salt out of your diet? One of the places these sneak in the most is in our condiments. Like our other fermented food recipes, this recipe takes advantage of fermentation as a preservation method, enhancing the nutritional value and extending shelf life without the use of any artificial preservatives. For a spicier mustard, use some black mustard seeds in combination with the yellow seeds.

It takes 3 days for the mustard to culture. We've put this recipe in the "everyday" category, as your time is required only at the beginning of this process.

For the vegan version of this recipe, use nondairy culture starter powder instead of Whey. We've put a list of our favorite brands in the "Resources" section on www.eatnakednow.com.

Makes 1 cup

½ **cup ground mustard**

2 **tablespoons whole yellow mustard seeds**

2 **tablespoons whole black or brown mustard seeds (optional)**

1 **teaspoon sea salt**

¼ **teaspoon granulated garlic**

1 **tablespoon lime juice**

2 **tablespoons Whey (page 63) or ½ packet nondairy culture starter powder**

Combine all ingredients except the Whey with ½ cup filtered water and stir with a spatula to form a paste. Add more water if necessary to reach desired consistency. Stir Whey thoroughly into the mustard.

Spoon mustard into a half-pint mason jar, pushing down the paste as you put it in the jar to make sure there are no air bubbles. Store at room temperature for 3 days to let it culture properly, and then store in the fridge. Will keep for up to several months.

CULTURED SALSA

Everyday •• Vegetarian, with vegan option •• Better than naked •• Make it once, use it lots

This is salsa cultured with Whey. As with some of the other cultured condiments such as Ketchup (page 66), Mustard (page 67), and Mayonnaise (page 71), the culturing works as a natural preservative without altering the flavor. We make this in big batches and keep it in the fridge.

As with many recipes in this chapter, it takes 2 days for the salsa to culture. We've put it in the "everyday" category, as your time is required only at the beginning of this process.

For the vegan version of this recipe, use nondairy culture starter powder instead of Whey. We've put a list of our favorite brands in the "Resources" section on www.eatnakednow.com.

Makes 4 cups

> 1 large carrot, coarsely chopped
>
> 2 cloves garlic, peeled
>
> ½ cup packed cilantro leaves
>
> 1 jalapeño pepper, seeded
>
> 1 red chile pepper, seeded (optional—use only for spicier salsas)
>
> Juice of 1 lime
>
> 1 (32-ounce) can fire-roasted tomatoes (or approximately 1½ pounds of fresh, peeled tomatoes), drained
>
> ½ teaspoon sea salt
>
> 2 tablespoons Whey (page 63) or ½ packet nondairy culture starter powder

Combine carrot, garlic, cilantro, and peppers in food processor. Pulse until minced. Add lime juice, tomatoes, and salt, pulsing several times to mix thoroughly.

Pour salsa into a medium bowl, add Whey, and stir to mix.

Put salsa into mason jars—either ½ quart or quart-size—leaving at least 1 inch between top of salsa and top of jar. Make sure the liquid is covering the vegetables. If it isn't, pour in a teeny bit of additional whey to cover the top of the salsa.

Put lids on jars and leave at room temperature for 2 days to culture. Store in the fridge. Keeps for up to a month.

TOMATO TECHNIQUES

How to peel tomatoes: Put the tomatoes to be peeled in a 5-quart pot, add enough cold water to cover them completely, and remove tomatoes. Bring water to a boil, then add some salt (about 1 teaspoon for every 8 cups of water). While waiting for water to boil, use a sharp paring knife to cut a small X on the bottom of each tomato (any variety of tomato works). Add tomatoes to boiling water, being careful not to overcrowd or stop the water from boiling. After a minute or two, you will see the skin of the tomato start to peel back at the x mark you cut into it. Remove the tomato immediately using a slotted spoon and place into a bowl filled with ice and cold water (an ice bath). Once all your tomatoes have cooled (approximately 5 minutes), remove them from the ice bath. You should be able to easily peel off the skins with your hands or a dry towel. If the skin is stubborn, carefully use a small paring knife, being sure not to squeeze the tomato.

How to seed a tomato: Once the tomato is peeled, cut it in half crosswise and squeeze each end over an empty bowl. You should see the seeds and juice filling the bowl. Just don't squeeze so hard that you demolish your lovely peeled tomato.

SPICY SALSA VERDE

Everyday •• Vegetarian, with vegan option •• Better than naked •• Make it once, use it lots

A nicely refreshing alternative to the usual red salsa, this salsa is made with tomatillos. Contrary to what many people think, tomatillos are not simply green tomatoes, they're a separate plant altogether. Eaten raw they're a little tart, but just lightly roasted they come to life. We pair this sauce with the Cheese Quesadilla (page 207) and Huevos Rancheros (page 86).

Like our Cultured Salsa (page 68), this sauce is cultured using Whey in order to preserve it longer. The process enhances its nutritional value, without affecting the flavor. We make this salsa in big batches and keep it in the fridge.

As with other recipes in this chapter, it takes 2 days for the salsa to culture. We've put it in the "everyday" category, as your time is required only at the beginning of this process.

For the vegan version of this recipe, use nondairy culture starter powder instead of Whey. We've put a list of our favorite brands in the "Resources" section on www.eatnakednow.com.

Makes 1½ cups

> ½ **onion, coarsely chopped**
>
> 6 **tomatillos, outer paper-like husk removed (approximately 10 ounces)**
>
> 1 **jalapeño pepper (seeded for milder salsa)**
>
> **Juice from** ½ **lime (approximately 1 tablespoon)**
>
> ½ **teaspoon sea salt**
>
> ¼ **packed cup chopped cilantro (optional)**
>
> 2 **tablespoons Whey (page 63) or** ½ **packet nondairy culture starter powder**

Preheat oven to 350°F. Spread out the onion, tomatillos (whole), and jalapeño pepper on an oven tray. Bake for 15 minutes.

Put ingredients from the oven into a high-powered blender. (If you don't want the salsa to be too spicy, cut the jalapeño peppers lengthwise and scoop out the seeds.) Add lime juice and sea salt. Pulse several times to blend the ingredients. Let cool. Stir in the cilantro and Whey once it's at room temperature.

Put salsa in a ½-quart mason jar, leaving at least 1 inch between top of salsa and top of jar. Make sure the liquid is covering the vegetables. If it isn't, pour in a teeny bit of additional whey to cover the top of the salsa.

Put lid on jar and leave at room temperature for 2 days to culture. Store in the fridge. Keeps for up to a month.

MAYONNAISE

Everyday •• Vegetarian •• Better than naked •• Make it once, use it lots

As with the other condiments in this book, we recommend making your own mayonnaise so you can control the quality of the ingredients, which is usually quite poor in commercially prepared mayonnaise. Most commercial mayonnaise uses low-quality and refined vegetable oils. This recipe uses only extra-virgin olive oil.

As with many of the other condiments in this book, we've added Whey, which naturally preserves the mayonnaise and extends its refrigerated shelf life from 1 to 2 weeks to several months. The culturing increases the nutritional content of the mayonnaise by adding enzymes and beneficial bacteria (probiotics). Because the mayonnaise cultures for only a short time, it doesn't affect the taste.

It takes 7 to 8 hours for the mayonnaise to culture. We've put this recipe in the "everyday" category, as your time is required only at the beginning of this process.

Makes 1½ cups

   2 whole eggs

   1 egg yolk

   ½ teaspoon sea salt

   1 cup extra-virgin olive oil

   1 tablespoon lemon juice

   1 teaspoon Dijon mustard (to make your own, see recipe on page 67)

   1 tablespoon Whey (page 63) or ½ packet nondairy culture starter powder

Crack 2 whole eggs into a small bowl and discard shells (or set them aside for making the Kitchen Scraps Veggie Stock on page 50). Add just the yolk from a third egg, and pour into a high-powered blender. Add sea salt and purée until smooth. With the blender still running, slowly add ¼ cup of the olive oil and continue to blend until smooth.

Add lemon juice, Dijon mustard, and Whey, and continue to purée. With the blender still running, slowly drizzle in the remaining olive oil. Blend on high until smooth and a little fluffy.

Pour into a glass jar and leave at room temperature for 7 to 8 hours to culture. If you're not using Whey, you can skip this step. Store, refrigerated, for up 2 weeks without the Whey or up to several months with the Whey.

SHEREE'S GREEN CULTURED VEGETABLES

Impress the neighbors •• Vegetarian, with vegan option •• Better than naked •• Make it once, use it lots

This cultured vegetable recipe was inspired by and named after a good friend of ours who makes exceptionally good cultured vegetables. This recipe is our attempt to reproduce one of her blends. It goes well with any protein or salad. Try adding a heaping spoonful with Fast and Easy Eggs and Greens (page 76), Kitchen Sink Breakfast (page 77), or Omega-Rich Arugula Salad (page 111).

If you use Whey as a culture starter, this recipe is vegetarian. For a vegan, dairy-free version, use a packet of nondairy culture starter. We've put a list of our favorite brands in the "Resources" section on www.eatnakednow.com.

Makes 8 cups

> 1 head green cabbage
>
> 2 large celery stalks, finely chopped
>
> 1 cup grated daikon radish
>
> 3 large kale leaves
>
> 1 tablespoon caraway seeds
>
> 4 tablespoons Whey (page 63) or 1 packet nondairy culture starter powder
>
> 2 teaspoons sea salt

Chop the green cabbage finely either by hand or with a food processor, and add to large mixing bowl. Add chopped celery and grated daikon radish to bowl. Finely chop the kale leaves and add to bowl. Add caraway seeds, Whey, and sea salt.

Using a meat pounder, the pestle from a mortar and pestle, or any heavy (waterproof), blunt object, pound the vegetables to release their juices. You'll need to pound for 4 to 5 minutes to get the juices really flowing.

Put veggies into 2 quart-size mason jars, compressing them as you go to make sure there are no air bubbles and to cover them completely in their juices. Be sure to leave at least 1 inch between the top of the veggies and the top of the jar.

Leave at room temperature for 3 to 5 days (3 days if it's summertime and your kitchen is warm; 5 days if it's wintertime and your kitchen is cooler) to culture. Transfer to cold storage. They last for several months. Each time you use them, be sure to compress the veggies in the jar before you put on the lid, to squeeze out any air bubbles.

SPICY SAUERKRAUT

Impress the neighbors •• Vegetarian, with vegan option •• Better than naked •• Make it once, use it lots

This sauerkraut has a little kick to it, which adds nicely to the sour flavor. This mix goes well with breakfasts and just about any protein. We rarely serve dinner without a scoop of some form of cultured vegetable. If you use Whey as a culture starter, this recipe is vegetarian. For a vegan, dairy-free version, use a packet of nondairy culture starter. We've put a list of our favorite brands in the "Resources" section on www.eatnakednow.com.

Makes 12 cups

- 1 head green cabbage
- 1 small head red cabbage
- 1 red bell pepper, seeded
- 1 jalapeño pepper (if you don't want it too spicy, remove the seeds)
- 8 radishes, grated
- 2 garlic cloves, minced
- 1 tablespoon sea salt
- 1 tablespoon red pepper flakes
- ¼ cup Whey (page 63) or 1 packet nondairy culture starter

Finely chop the cabbages and peppers either by hand or with a food processor, and add to a large mixing bowl. Add the grated radish and minced garlic to the bowl. Mix well. Add the sea salt, red pepper flakes, and Whey.

Using a meat pounder, the pestle from a mortar and pestle, or any heavy (waterproof), blunt object, pound the vegetables to release their juices, mixing well. You'll need to pound for 4 to 5 minutes to get the juices really flowing.

Put veggies into three widemouthed quart-size mason jars, compressing them as you go to make sure there are no air bubbles and to cover them completely in their juices. Be sure to leave at least 1 inch between the top of the veggies and the top of the jar.

Leave at room temperature for 3 to 5 days (3 days if it's summertime and your kitchen is warm; 5 days if it's wintertime and your kitchen is cooler) to ferment. Transfer to cold storage. They last for several months. Each time you use them, be sure to compress the veggies in the jar before you put on the lid, to squeeze out any air bubbles.

7
Breakfasts

Breakfast is the most important meal of the day. Unfortunately, it's also the meal that most often gets skipped. Eating a proper breakfast can be the difference between consistent energy and a pattern of energy spikes and crashes. Skipping it can be the reason for those after-dinner sugar cravings and that feeling of insatiability later on in the day. Don't underestimate it. We recommend that you eat within an hour or, even better, a half hour of waking.

Many breakfasts are dominated by starchy carbohydrates—cereals, toast, fruit, a bagel. You'll notice that a lot of our breakfast recipes are more rooted in protein and vegetables. When we recommend that people eat vegetables for breakfast we're often met with confusion. Well, we've got several recipes in here that will show you how easy it is to do. It's a rare day when breakfast at our house doesn't include some kind of vegetable. Starting the day with this kind of breakfast will give you an even energy and will keep you fuller longer. You might even be able to skip your morning snack and make it all the way to lunch without needing more food.

FAST AND EASY EGGS AND GREENS

In a rush •• Vegetarian •• Better than naked

This is one of Margaret's go-to recipes when she's got minimal time for food prep in the morning. It takes little time to make and provides a fully balanced meal with some good green veggies, protein, and a little fat. The optional cultured veggies make this breakfast extremely digestible and add a nice flavor punch to start your day.

Makes 1 serving

2 eggs

1 packed cup chopped kale

½ teaspoon Cultured Butter (page 64) or organic butter

2 tablespoons Sheree's Green Cultured Vegetables (page 72) or Spicy Sauerkraut (page 74)

Sea salt

Freshly ground pepper

Fill a small saucepan two-thirds full with water, cover, and bring to a boil over high heat. Using a spoon, gently put the eggs, shells still on, into the water and set a timer for 6 minutes. Eggs should be fully covered with water. Allow eggs to boil on high heat, covered.

Put the kale in a small steamer basket designed to fit the saucepan, or improvise with a small heat-resistant steel colander or sieve. With 2 to 3 minutes of cooking time left on the eggs, place the steamer basket of kale above the boiling water and replace the lid. The kale will steam using the water that's boiling the eggs.

When the 6-minute timer goes off, remove kale and eggs from heat. Put kale in a bowl and set aside. Run eggs under cold water and peel. Put the peeled eggs in the bowl with the kale, add the butter and cultured veggies, and mash the eggs and veggies together with a fork. Season to taste with salt and pepper, and serve.

KITCHEN SINK BREAKFAST

In a rush •• Vegetarian •• Better than naked

This is less of a recipe than a formula for a quick and dirty breakfast. Essentially, you take leftovers from a previous dinner or lunch, heat them up, and top them with two eggs done in your favorite style. We recommend adding a scoop of cultured vegetables to help with the digestibility.

Makes 2 servings

> **2 cups leftover vegetables of any type, cooked or raw**
>
> **½ cup leftover beans of any type, cooked**
>
> **4 eggs**
>
> **¼ cup Sheree's Green Cultured Vegetables (page 72) or Spicy Sauerkraut (page 74)**

In a small saucepan, reheat the leftover vegetables and beans over medium heat. Be careful not to overcook them. This should take only 2 to 3 minutes but will depend on how the vegetables were prepared to begin with.

While the veggies and beans are warming up, cook the eggs in a separate pan or pot in your favorite way: fried, scrambled, poached, or boiled.

To serve, divide the vegetables and beans between two plates, and top with 2 cooked eggs per plate and a scoop of cultured vegetables.

WAKE-UP SHAKE

In a rush •• Vegan •• Better than naked

This recipe takes advantage of our frozen banana trick, mentioned in chapter 2. We peel our bananas and store them in a freezer bag or plastic container in the freezer, keeping them ready for smoothies at a moment's notice. We suggest using frozen berries, but if the berries are in season, fresh is fine too. We also include bee pollen as an option. Bee pollen is considered a superfood because it's enzyme rich and packed with vitamins (especially B vitamins) and phytochemicals.

Makes 1 serving

- 1 frozen banana
- 2 tablespoons soaked almonds or 1 tablespoon almond butter
- ½ cup frozen blueberries
- 2 pitted dates
- ¼ teaspoon cinnamon
- 1 tablespoon flaxseed oil
- ½ cup store-bought or homemade Coconut Milk (page 44)
- ½ teaspoon vanilla extract
- 1 teaspoon bee pollen (optional)
- ½ cup filtered water or coconut water

Combine all ingredients in the blender and blend until smooth. Drink immediately for highest nutrient content.

GREEN SMOOTHIE

In a rush •• Vegan •• Raw •• Better than naked

This smoothie is a great way to get more greens into your life and, despite the color, is absolutely delicious. We've had many clients who resisted any kind of green drink but ended up loving this smoothie. Ideally use a high-end professional blender, but if you don't have one, any good blender will do. We've included ingredient options for those of you using a normal blender.

For the most naked version of this smoothie, use the water and flesh of a young green coconut instead of the coconut water and cashews. Nothing beats the water straight out of the coconut.

Makes 2 servings

1 head romaine lettuce, stem chopped off

½ cup peeled, coarsely chopped cucumber

1 to 2 cups coconut water (depending on how thick you like your smoothie)

½ packed cup fresh parsley

Juice of 1 lime

¼ cup cashews, presoaked overnight (alternately, if you're not using a professional blender, use 2 tablespoons of unsweetened raw cashew butter)

½ avocado, fresh scooped out and pit discarded

Combine all ingredients in your blender, and blend until smooth. You may need to pulse the blender a few times to get it started, and you'll need to use the manufacturer-provided "wand" or a wooden spoon to push the bits down into the blade for proper mixing. If you're using a wooden spoon, be very careful not to hit the blades as they're spinning. Drink immediately for highest nutrient content.

ORANGE CREAMSICLE SMOOTHIE

In a rush •• Vegan •• Better than naked

One of the fondest memories of James's childhood is the sound of the ice cream truck cruising through the neighborhood followed by kids sprinting to catch it and buy a treat. The flavor that most represents these warm summer days is the orange Creamsicle. Here's a morning smoothie that reproduces that flavor with some good nutritional value added and without the refined sugar.

Makes 2 servings

> **Juice and zest of 1 large orange (approximately ½ cup)**
>
> **½ teaspoon vanilla extract**
>
> **½ cup soaked cashews**
>
> **3 to 5 dates (depending on size), pitted (use only if you've got a good blender) or 1 tablespoon raw honey**
>
> **4 to 5 ice cubes**
>
> **¾ cup store-bought or homemade Coconut Milk (page 44)**
>
> **½ cup water or coconut water**

Combine all ingredients in a high-powered blender, and blend on high until smooth. You may need to pulse the blender a few times to make sure the ice has been crushed fully. Drink immediately for highest nutrient content.

HOLIDAY PUMPKIN SMOOTHIE

In a rush •• Vegetarian, with vegan option

Why wait for the holidays to eat pumpkin pie? This smoothie has that same rich flavor but in drinkable breakfast form, without all the refined sugars and flours. If you're using pumpkin purée from a can, make sure it contains no ingredients other than pumpkin.

For a vegan version of this smoothie, substitute coconut milk and water for the raw milk, and omit the egg.

Makes 2 servings

> 1 cup precooked winter squash, such as butternut squash, pumpkin, or kabocha, or 1 cup canned unsweetened organic pumpkin purée
>
> ½ cup store-bought or homemade whole Coconut Milk (page 44)
>
> 1 cup raw milk (if you don't have access to quality unpasteurized milk, or want the smoothie to be vegan, then replace with another ½ cup whole coconut milk and ½ cup water or coconut water)
>
> 1 egg (omit if you don't have access to quality pastured eggs, or if you want the smoothie to be vegan)
>
> 4 to 5 pitted dates (depending on size)
>
> ½ teaspoon vanilla extract
>
> 1 tablespoon maple syrup (ideally grade B, even better grade C)
>
> ¼ teaspoon ground nutmeg
>
> ¼ teaspoon ground cinnamon
>
> ⅛ teaspoon ground clove
>
> ⅛ teaspoon grated ginger (optional)
>
> 4 ice cubes

Combine all ingredients in a high-powered blender, and blend on high until smooth. You may need to pulse the blender a few times to make sure the ice has been crushed fully. Drink immediately for highest nutrient content.

FLORENTINE OMELET WITH A TWIST

Everyday •• Vegetarian

This is our twist on the Florentine omelet. Instead of spinach, which is overused and has oxalic acid (an antinutrient that inhibits your body's ability to absorb minerals and is the source of that squeaky feeling on your teeth when you eat lots of spinach), it uses kale. Instead of your standard white or crimini mushrooms, it uses shiitakes, for a slightly Asian feel. The sun-dried tomatoes are a nice touch to make the flavor pop.

Makes 2 servings

> 1 tablespoon plus 2 teaspoons butter or ghee
>
> 3 to 4 shiitake mushrooms, sliced lengthwise (about 1 cup)
>
> ⅛ teaspoon sea salt
>
> 2 sun-dried tomatoes, julienned
>
> 2 cups finely chopped kale
>
> 4 eggs
>
> Pinch freshly ground pepper
>
> 1 tablespoon grated Parmesan

Heat 1 tablespoon of the butter in a small skillet over medium heat. When melted, add the mushrooms and salt, and cook for 2 to 3 minutes, until just soft. Add the sun-dried tomatoes and kale, which might still be a little wet from being washed—this is fine, it will help it steam. Cook for 2 more minutes. Remove all veggies from heat, and put on a plate.

Using the same skillet, melt the remaining 1 teaspoon butter. Break 2 eggs into a bowl, and whisk together lightly with a fork. When butter has melted pour the whisked eggs into the pan, adding a pinch of freshly ground pepper. As the eggs cook, sprinkle with half of the Parmesan cheese and use your spatula to fold up the edges and let the uncooked egg on top run to the bottom of the pan. Flip the eggs to cook the other side. Put on a plate and set aside while you repeat these steps for the next 2 eggs. (If you don't know how to make an omelet, visit www. eatnakednow.com/videos and search "omelet" for a video on how to make a basic omelet.)

Put half of the kale and mushroom mixture onto one half of the omelet, and fold the egg over it. Sprinkle with a little more Parmesan cheese and serve warm.

Note about sun-dried tomatoes: We prefer to get our sun-dried tomatoes dry, not packed in any oil. If your sun-dried tomatoes are extremely hard, you'll need to reconstitute them by soaking them in warm water for 10 to 15 minutes. If they're a little soft and chewy, you can use them as is, without reconstituting.

CURRIED EGG SCRAMBLE

Everyday •• Vegetarian

Curry is a spice most people wouldn't associate with breakfast, but this savory dish is flavorful without being overpowering. It's also a great way to creatively get more vegetables in your morning meal.

Makes 2 servings

  1 tablespoon plus 1 teaspoon butter or ghee

  4 eggs

  ¼ yellow or red onion, thinly sliced (about ¼ cup)

  5 crimini mushrooms, sliced (about ½ cup)

  ½ teaspoon salt

  ½ teaspoon ground turmeric

  1 teaspoon curry powder

  ½ teaspoon chili powder

  ½ teaspoon paprika

  ¼ cup grated carrots

  4 mini tomatoes, quartered

  1 small zucchini, diced (about ¼ cup)

  1 cup spinach

  ⅛ teaspoon freshly ground pepper

In a large skillet, melt 1 tablespoon of butter. While the butter is melting, crack eggs in a small bowl and scramble with a fork. Set eggs aside.

When the pan is hot but not smoking, add onions, mushrooms, and salt, and sauté for 2 minutes, until just soft. Add turmeric, curry, chili powder, and paprika to mixture, and mix well.

Add carrots, tomatoes, zucchini, and spinach, and cook for 2 to 3 minutes, until moist. Remove cooked veggies from heat, put into a separate bowl, and set aside.

Wipe pan with a clean towel and place back over medium heat. Add remaining 1 teaspoon butter. When pan is hot, but not smoking, add eggs. Allow eggs to set a little then add cooked veggies on top of the eggs. Using a heat-resistant spatula, scramble eggs and veggie mix to desired consistency.

Plate the eggs, sprinkle with pepper, and serve warm.

SWEET POTATO BREAKFAST HASH

Impress the neighbors •• Omnivore

This is a delicious breakfast hash that's a nice switch from eggs. When you're buying the sausage, look for nitrate- and sugar-free sausage, ideally made from pastured chickens, turkeys, or pork. This is, admittedly, hard to find. The most important thing is the quality of the meat that went into the sausage, so prioritize finding sausage from pastured or at least organic chickens. If you can find that and a nitrate-free sausage, you're doing great. Sugar-free might be asking too much, but see whether you can find it. Your best bet is at the farmers market.

Makes 3 servings

1½ tablespoons ghee or lard

½ teaspoon sea salt

½ teaspoon freshly ground black pepper

½ teaspoon paprika

½ teaspoon ground cumin

½ teaspoon chili powder

2 sweet potatoes, cubed (2 to 2½ cups)

½ onion, diced (approximately ½ cup)

¼ red bell pepper, diced (approximately ¼ cup)

¼ yellow bell pepper, diced (approximately ¼ cup)

2 stalks celery, diced (approximately ½ cup)

2 cups chopped kale

3 chicken, turkey, or pork sausage links, cut into ½-inch-thick half moons

Preheat oven to 385°F. Place an oven tray in the oven as it preheats, along with a large heat-resistant mixing bowl with the ghee in it to melt.

When the ghee has melted, remove from oven and add the salt, black pepper, paprika, cumin, and chili powder to the bowl, mixing well. Add the sweet potatoes, onion, red and yellow peppers, and celery. Toss well to coat the veggies thoroughly in the ghee and spice mixture. Pull the heated oven tray out of the oven, spread the veggies on it, and bake for 15 minutes.

At the 15-minute mark pull the veggies out of the oven, add the kale and sausage, stir to mix them in, and then put back into the oven for another 15 to 17 minutes, until hash has lightly browned. Serve warm.

HUEVOS RANCHEROS

Everyday •• Vegetarian •• Better than naked

This is our version of one of Margaret's favorite Mexican egg breakfasts. It's got a few more vegetables than you'd typically find, and we mix it up by using Spicy Salsa Verde instead of your usual salsa (although feel free to use the Cultured Salsa recipe on page 68 if you prefer). We poach the eggs, but if you're not a fan of this style of egg, feel free to fry or scramble them.

Makes 2 servings

- 2 sprouted corn tortillas (see the "Resources" section on www.eatnakednow.com for our favorite brands and sources)
- 4 tablespoons grated cheese (Monterey jack, cheddar, or feta)
- 1 cup chopped arugula
- ¼ cup presoaked and precooked black beans (if using canned, use a low-sodium variety and drain and rinse them well)
- 1 teaspoon plain white vinegar
- 4 eggs
- ¼ cup Spicy Salsa Verde (page 70)
- ½ avocado, sliced lengthwise into strips

In a large and deep skillet or medium saucepan, heat 2 inches of water over high heat for poaching the eggs. While the water is heating, heat a separate small skillet over medium heat. Add 1 of the tortillas, 1 tablespoon of the cheese, half of the arugula, and half of the black beans.

When the water in the large skillet has come to a slow boil, turn down the heat to medium and add the vinegar. Carefully crack the first 2 eggs into the poaching water, discarding the shells. The eggs should be ready in 2 to 4 minutes, depending on how runny you like your eggs. To test the eggs, poke them gently with the back of a spoon. The firmer they are, the more cooked. (For a video demonstration of how to poach eggs, visit www.eatnakednow.com/videos and search for "poached eggs.")

Spoon the eggs out of the poaching water using a slotted spoon, let water drain off of them, and put them on the tortilla. Sprinkle a second tablespoon of cheese onto the eggs. Top them with half of the Spicy Salsa Verde and half of the avocado slices.

Repeat with the second tortilla and remaining ingredients. Serve immediately.

AMARANTH PORRIDGE

Everyday •• Vegetarian, with vegan option

Amaranth is a gluten-free grain that doesn't get a lot of press (unlike quinoa or millet) but packs some serious nutritional punch. You can find it at most health food stores, or see the "Resources" section on www.eatnakednow.com for our favorite brands. It has an unusually high amount of protein for a grain, without the problems of gluten. We've also added in some buckwheat, which, despite "wheat" being in its name, is also gluten-free.

You might wonder at the addition of the butter. This is to provide the longer, steadier-burn fuel that fat provides, and to reduce the blood sugar spike that comes from a carbohydrate-heavy breakfast.

For a vegan version of this recipe, substitute coconut oil for butter.

Makes 4 servings

   1 cup amaranth

   ¼ cup buckwheat

   ½ green apple, cored and chopped

   1 stick cinnamon

   1 tablespoon butter or unrefined coconut oil

   2 tablespoons maple syrup

In a medium saucepan, combine all ingredients except maple syrup. Add 3 cups water. Cover and bring to a boil. Once boiling, turn down the heat to low and let cook, still covered, for 25 minutes. Mix well and serve warm with ½ tablespoon of maple syrup drizzled over top of each serving.

GRAINLESS GRANOLA

Everyday •• *Vegan* •• *Better than naked* •• *Make it once, use it lots*

Store-bought cereals are one of the places where a lot of un-naked ingredients hide. Even the healthier options tend to have too much sugar and use grains that aren't properly prepared. We've created a grainless granola you can feel good about, and that goes really well with Yogurt (page 65). Add some fresh berries in summertime and you've got a delicious and easy breakfast. We also use this as the topping for our Berry Cobbler (page 246).

Makes 3 to 4 cups

- **2 cups almonds, ideally presoaked and dehydrated or slow-roasted**
- **½ cup golden hunza raisins or unsweetened dried fruit of choice (apricots, apples, and pears work well)**
- **1 cup sunflower seeds, ideally presoaked and dehydrated or slow-roasted**
- **¼ cup whole flaxseeds**
- **¼ cup ground flaxseeds**
- **¼ cup ground hemp seeds**
- **Meat from 1 young green coconut (approximately ½ packed cup) or ½ cup dried unsweetened coconut flakes**
- **⅓ cup maple syrup (grade C is ideal but hard to find, grade B is next best)**
- **1 teaspoon cinnamon**
- **¼ teaspoon sea salt**

Preheat oven to 350°F. While oven is preheating, combine almonds, raisins, seeds, and coconut in a food processor and pulse repeatedly to blend until the mixture attains a granola-like consistency. Put into a big mixing bowl and add maple syrup, cinnamon, and salt. Using a spatula, mix well.

Line an oven tray with a piece of parchment paper, and spread granola out loosely over the tray. Bake for 15 to 20 minutes, until slightly browned and dried. Let cool, and store in a glass container in the fridge or freezer until ready to use. Keeps for 1 month in fridge and 3 months in the freezer.

BROILED GRAPEFRUIT

Everyday •• Vegetarian

This is a family favorite at Margaret's house, and it's how we always start our Christmas morning. It's a bit of a sugar load to start your day, so we don't recommend it for more than the most special occasion—it is scrumptious. Don't be shy to squeeze and drink the juices out of the grapefruit rind after you've eaten it. It's messy but worth it. Followed by Portobello Eggs Benedict (page 90), this makes one delicious gourmet breakfast.

Makes 4 servings

> **2 large grapefruits (Ruby Reds work well, but any variety is fine)**
>
> **4 teaspoons butter**
>
> **4 tablespoons maple sugar (you can also use maple syrup, but the sugar is best because it doesn't run off)**

Preheat oven to broil. Cut each grapefruit in half crosswise. Segment it by running a paring knife along the membrane perimeter of each segment. Leave the segments in the rind. Dot the open face of each grapefruit half with 1 teaspoon of the butter, and drizzle each open face with 1 tablespoon of the maple sugar or syrup.

Put grapefruit on oven tray, face up, and broil on high for 10 to 12 minutes. If your broiler is in the main part of your oven, make sure you put the grapefruit on one of the top racks so that it's close to the broiler. The grapefruit will brown on top.

Put each grapefruit half in its own bowl, and pour any juices from the pan over top. Serve warm.

PORTOBELLO EGGS BENEDICT

Impress the neighbors •• Omnivore, with vegetarian option

This is a fun, bread-free, and healthier spin on the classic eggs bennie. We've replaced the English muffin with a portobello mushroom and the ham with spinach, and we use our Vegan Hollandaise Sauce—lighter and less finicky than the traditional version—to finish it off. We use a little lard on the mushrooms to give it a hint of the flavor you'd have with the ham, but if you don't have lard on hand, or to keep this recipe vegetarian, you can also use ghee or butter.

Makes 2 servings

> **2 large portobello mushrooms, stemmed (or 4 small ones, if the large aren't available)**
>
> **½ teaspoon lard or ghee**
>
> **Pinch sea salt**
>
> **Pinch freshly ground pepper**
>
> **2 firmly packed cups baby spinach**
>
> **1 teaspoon white vinegar**
>
> **4 eggs**
>
> **1 recipe Vegan Hollandaise Sauce (page 153)**
>
> **Pinch paprika**

Preheat oven to 385°F.

Lightly rub underside of portobello mushrooms with lard. Place on an oven tray with underside facing up and cook for 20 to 25 minutes, until soft with some of the liquids released into the mushroom cap. Sprinkle with salt and pepper.

While the mushrooms are cooking, lightly rinse the spinach to remove any dirt, leaving the leaves a little wet. You don't need to dry it—the extra water will help to steam the spinach. Heat a large sauté pan over medium heat. Add wet spinach leaves, cover, and let the leaves wilt. This will happen in 2 to 3 minutes, so stay close. Remove the spinach from heat, put it in a small bowl, and set aside.

Fill the same pan you used to steam the spinach with 2 inches of water. Add vinegar. Bring the water to a slow boil over medium-high heat. Gently drop the eggs into the water one at a time, and poach for 3 to 4 minutes, until they reach the desired firmness when you press them with the back of a spoon. (For a video demonstration of how to poach eggs, visit www.eatnakednow.com/videos and search for "poached eggs.")

To plate your Portobello Eggs Benedict, place each mushroom on its own plate, underside facing up. Put half of the wilted spinach on top of each mushroom, as a bed for 2 poached eggs. Top with the Vegan Hollandaise Sauce and a pinch of paprika.

APPLE PANCAKES

Impress the neighbors •• Vegetarian

These are not your normal everyday pancakes. These pancakes are made to impress. This recipe makes substantial and rather fancy pancakes. We prefer to make them in a small skillet and keep them heated as we make each one individually, but that does extend the prep time. You can also make one large pancake and cut it up into smaller portions, but the visual effect isn't as good. This recipe uses a combination of sorghum flour, corn flour, and buckwheat flour to replace the wheat flour typically used. You can find these gluten-free flours in most health food stores or the gluten-free aisle of your supermarket, or visit the "Resources" section at www.eatnakednow.com for our favorite brands and places to order them online.

Makes 4 pancakes

2 green apples

1 cup unsweetened apple juice

1 tablespoon ground cinnamon

Lemon wedge

1 cup sorghum flour

½ cup corn flour

½ cup buckwheat flour

½ teaspoon baking soda

¼ teaspoon sea salt

2 eggs

3 tablespoons maple syrup

1½ cups store-bought or homemade Buttermilk (page 64)

½ teaspoon vanilla extract (optional)

2 to 3 teaspoons butter

Preheat oven to 350°F.

Peel and core the apples, and cut them into ¼-inch-thick wedges. Do your best to slice them evenly. Put apple wedges in a small saucepan along with apple juice, 1½ cups water, ½ teaspoon of the cinnamon, and lemon wedge. Cover and bring to a boil. Remove from heat and let stand, covered, for 2 to 5 minutes, until soft.

While the apples are cooking, make the batter by combining sorghum flour, corn flour, buckwheat flour, baking soda, ½ teaspoon of the cinnamon, and salt in a large mixing bowl. Stir to mix all dry ingredients.

Crack eggs into a separate small bowl. Add 1 tablespoon of maple syrup, buttermilk, and vanilla, and whisk well to mix with the eggs. Whisk together dry and wet batter ingredients. Because it's gluten-free, you don't have to worry about overmixing.

When apples have finished cooking, pour off liquid into a small saucepan. Add 2 tablespoons of maple syrup. Put on stove, uncovered, on high heat, to reduce down to a syrup. Takes approximately 20 minutes.

While sauce is reducing, heat 1 teaspoon of the butter in a small ovenproof skillet. As soon as butter has melted, turn off heat. Arrange one-fourth of the apple wedges fanned out in a starburst formation on the bottom of the pan. Pour ½- to ¾ cup of batter into skillet with apples, making sure to completely cover the apple wedges. Turn heat back on and cook for 2 to 3 minutes on low-medium heat to cook the bottom of the pancake. Put in the oven to bake for approximately 8 minutes, until set.

Turn cooked pancake out of pan onto an oven tray. Because the pan was buttered, it should pop right out. Cover to keep warm. Repeat last steps for all 4 pancakes.

Put each pancake on its own plate, place 1 to 2 apple wedges on the center of the pancake, drizzle apple syrup on top, and sprinkle with remaining cinnamon. Serve warm.

CRUSTLESS MINI-QUICHES

Impress the neighbors •• Vegetarian •• Make it once, use it lots

This recipe makes use of muffin tins to make tiny quiches—delightful for an elegant Sunday brunch, or double the recipe and store them in the refrigerator for use as grab-and-go breakfasts throughout the week. They're crustless, so there's no fiddling with dough or worrying about gluten alternatives. Once you've got this recipe down, experiment with different vegetable combinations.

Makes 6 to 8 mini-quiches or 4 large quiche muffins

2 tablespoons ghee or butter

2 tablespoons finely diced onion

⅛ teaspoon sea salt

½ cup sliced mushrooms

2 tablespoons finely diced red bell pepper

1 cup spinach or arugula

4 eggs

1 tablespoon grated Parmesan cheese (optional)

Preheat oven to 350°F. Use 1 tablespoon of the ghee to grease 8 cups of a 24-count mini muffin tin or 4 cups in a 12-count muffin tin.

Heat the remaining 1 tablespoon ghee in a medium saucepan. Sauté onions over medium heat for 2 to 3 minutes, until translucent, adding a pinch of salt as they're cooking. Add mushrooms and sauté for another 2 to 3 minutes, until soft. Add red pepper and half of the spinach, and continue to cook for another 2 to 3 minutes, until spinach becomes bright green. Empty pan ingredients into a bowl and allow to cool.

Crack eggs into a bowl, mixing well with a fork. Add cheese and slightly cooled vegetables, mixing lightly. Fill the muffin cups about three-fourths full with egg mixture. Make sure there's an equal amount of the vegetable mixture in each muffin cup.

Bake quiche "muffins" for approximately 10 to 12 minutes. The quiches will start to puff up a little (although not as much as a real muffin) and brown on top. As soon as egg is solid, remove pan from the oven, allowing it to cool briefly. Using a knife or mini spatula, remove the quiches from the muffin cups and serve warm on top of a bed of the remaining spinach.

8
Salads and Sides

I t's no accident that the largest section of recipes in this book is the "Salads and Sides" chapter. Vegetables are the foundation of any naked diet, and, in our opinion, you can't get too many of them. We've included many different and creative ways to add more vegetables to just about any meal.

While other sections make good use of the "make it once, use it lots" principle, you'll find this chapter doesn't do that quite as much. Produce starts to break down quickly as soon as you cut it, so, with only a few exceptions, the more you're able to prepare your salads as you eat them, the better.

What will make the preparation time of these salads much more manageable is to make one or two dressings from the "Sauces, Dressings, and Dips" chapter on the weekend, and then use them several times throughout the week. This will significantly reduce the time it takes to make these dishes.

Most of the recipes in this section are vegan or vegetarian. We like to start with a big salad or veggie side, and then add whatever meat we're eating to it. This ensures that the vegetables are the main feature of the meal.

KALE ARAME SALAD

In a rush •• Vegan

This is a great introduction to cooking with a naked superfood: seaweed. If you're new to cooking with seaweed, arame is one of the best seaweeds to start with, as it doesn't have the slimy texture associated with some of the other varieties. You can find arame at your local Asian market or most health food stores. This salad makes an excellent companion to any seared fish, such as Sesame-Crusted Salmon (page 175) or Seared Tuna (page 171).

Makes 2 servings

¼ **cup dried arame**

Cold filtered water

1 big bunch kale, washed, stemmed, and chopped

1 tablespoon toasted sesame oil

2 teaspoons gluten-free tamari soy sauce

1 teaspoon freshly squeezed lemon juice

1 to 2 teaspoons sesame seeds

Put arame in a small bowl and cover with cold filtered water. Set aside to soak while you're preparing the kale.

In a large stockpot over medium heat, add washed kale (still wet). Using tongs, toss and turn the kale as it's cooking, until it turns a bright green and wilts slightly. This takes about 2 minutes. You may need to add a few tablespoons of water if the kale wasn't wet enough from the washing. Be careful not to overcook it. Drain in a colander and set aside.

Drain the arame. In a mixing bowl, combine arame, sesame oil, tamari, and lemon juice. Add the steamed kale and toss. Sprinkle with sesame seeds and toss some more.

Serve warm, or refrigerate and eat cold later.

EGGPLANT BASIL SALAD

In a rush •• Vegetarian

This simple salad is an excellent late-summer dish when eggplant is in season and fresh basil is abundant. You can eat this salad warm or cold, depending on your taste. It makes an excellent side dish for Nut-Crusted Pesto Chicken (page 187). You can substitute your favorite cheese for the mozzarella. To make this salad particularly decadent, substitute burrata for the mozzarella cheese, if you can find it.

You'll notice this recipe uses both butter and olive oil for sautéing the eggplant. The butter, a saturated fatty acid, protects the more delicate olive oil, a monounsaturated fatty acid, from the heat of cooking. This is a great trick when you want the Mediterranean flavor of olive oil, but don't want the heat to damage it.

Makes 4 servings

> 1 tablespoon extra-virgin olive oil
>
> 1 tablespoon butter
>
> 1 large eggplant
>
> ¼ teaspoon sea salt
>
> 2 tablespoons julienned sun-dried tomato
>
> ½ cup fresh basil leaves
>
> Zest from 1 large lemon (approximately 1 tablespoon)
>
> 4 ounces fresh mozzarella cheese, cut into ½-inch dice

Heat olive oil and butter in a large skillet over medium heat. While oil is heating, cut eggplant into ½-inch cubes. Toss cubed eggplant with salt, mixing it well with your hands. The salt brings out some of the moisture in the eggplant. Sauté eggplant for 2 to 3 minutes, until just tender. Add the sun-dried tomatoes and 2 tablespoons filtered water, cover the pan, and sauté for another 2 to 3 minutes.

Toss the sautéed eggplant and sun-dried tomatoes with the basil, lemon zest, and mozzarella cheese. Serve warm, or refrigerate and serve cold.

Note about sun-dried tomatoes: We prefer to get our sun-dried tomatoes dry, not packed in any oil. If your sun-dried tomatoes are extremely hard, you'll need to reconstitute them by soaking them in warm water for 10 to 15 minutes. If they're a little soft and chewy, you can use them as is, without reconstituting.

UMEBOSHI BROCCOLI

In a rush •• Vegan •• Better than naked

This recipe takes steamed broccoli (bor-riiing) to a whole new level. We toss it with Umeboshi Dressing and sprinkle it with red pepper flakes, and suddenly the dish comes alive.

Remember not to steam the broccoli for too long. Once it turns bright green (2 to 3 minutes), it's ready. As soon as it starts to go a dull shade of green, it's overcooked.

Makes 4 servings

> **3 cups chopped broccoli (use both the florets and stems)**
>
> **2 tablespoons Umeboshi Dressing (page 143)**
>
> **¼ teaspoon red pepper flakes**

Heat a large skillet on high heat. When hot, add the broccoli and ¼ cup water. Cover it with a lid immediately, and let steam for 2 to 3 minutes, until broccoli has turned a bright green and is still firm.

Remove from heat and drain the broccoli. In a mixing bowl, toss the broccoli with the Umeboshi Dressing. Sprinkle with red pepper flakes and serve warm.

MELON CUCUMBER SALAD

In a rush •• Vegan •• Raw

This salad is nicely cooling, ideal for summer. If you're in a really big rush, use precut melon instead of cutting it yourself. It's a little less naked, but it works in a pinch.

Makes 6 servings

> 1 honeydew melon
>
> 2 kiwis, peeled and cut into thin half moons
>
> ½ small cucumber, diced (about ½ cup)
>
> 5 to 7 mint leaves, roughly shredded
>
> ⅛ to ¼ cup **Creamy Mint Magic Dressing** (page 136)

Halve and then quarter the melon. Spoon out the seeds and discard. Cut the flesh of the melon into 1-inch squares, cutting just to the rind, but not cutting through the rind. Cut the rind off the melon squares and put them in a bowl (for a video demonstration of this technique, visit www.eatnakednow.com/videos). There should be approximately 4 cups of cubed melon.

Add kiwi, cucumber, and mint leaves. Pour dressing over top and stir well to coat. Serve immediately or, even better, chill and serve cold.

CUBAN GREEN PEAS

In a rush •• Vegetarian, with vegan option

This is a fast and easy winter dish, making use of frozen peas. Frozen vegetables are great in winter when fresh produce isn't available. If you have leftovers, turn them into a really easy Creamy Tarragon Pea Soup (page 160).

For a vegan version of this recipe, substitute coconut oil for ghee.

Makes 4 to 6 servings

1 tablespoon ghee or unrefined coconut oil

½ teaspoon granulated garlic

1 teaspoon ground cumin

¼ teaspoon red pepper flakes

Pinch sea salt

1 pound frozen green peas

Melt ghee in a large skillet over medium heat. Add garlic, cumin, red pepper flakes, and sea salt to ghee as it's melting. Add peas and stir to mix with ghee and spices. Add 1 tablespoon filtered water, cover, and cook for 5 minutes, just until peas have warmed and turned a bright green. If the peas go a dull shade of green, they've been overcooked.

Serve warm.

WATERCRESS SALAD

In a rush •• Vegan •• Raw

Watercress is a fresh and unusual lettuce, available only at certain times of the year. It's a wonderfully cooling green to use during the summer. We've kept this recipe simple, since the greens have so much flavor and combine leaves and stalks. If you eat fish, we recommend this dish with Smelt Fry (page 179). The flavors complement each other well.

Makes 4 servings

> 1 bunch watercress (approximately 5 to 6 cups)
>
> 1 carrot, grated
>
> 4 red radishes, grated
>
> 2 tablespoons Umeboshi Dressing (page 143) or Carrot Ginger Dressing (page 149)

Chop off and discard ends of watercress stalk, and tear watercress into big chunks using your hands. In a large salad bowl, toss the watercress with the grated carrot and radishes. Just before serving, toss salad with the Umeboshi Dressing.

CURRIED SWISS CHARD WITH ALMONDS

In a rush •• Vegetarian •• Better than naked

Swiss chard is a delicious green, and it goes particularly well with any fish dish. The addition of almonds along with the curry dressing is a really nice touch. It's a really fast and easy recipe. We recommend that you pair it with Broiled Sardines (page 176) or Seared Tuna (page 171).

Makes 4 servings

> **1 bunch Swiss chard, including stalk**
>
> **½ cup whole or presliced almonds, ideally presoaked and dehydrated or slow-roasted**
>
> **2 tablespoons In a Hurry Curry Dressing (page 135)**

Wash and coarsely chop the Swiss chard, leaving some of the water on the leaves. If you're using whole almonds, coarsely chop them with a knife. Heat a medium saucepan over medium heat. Put chard and almonds in pot, and cook for 2 to 3 minutes, stirring continually with a set of tongs. Cook only until just wilted. The stalks should still be slightly firm. Don't overcook.

Remove from heat and toss with In a Hurry Curry Dressing. Serve immediately.

SPEEDY GREEN SALAD

In a rush •• Vegetarian, with vegan option

This uncomplicated salad is a good example of how easy it can be to eat more vegetables. What keeps most people from eating more vegetables is the perception that it takes too long to prepare them. We want to show how quickly you can toss together some simple ingredients to make something healthy and yummy.

For a vegan version of this recipe, omit the Parmesan.

Makes 4 servings

> **4 cups mixed green lettuce (any variety works)**
>
> **1 small carrot, grated (approximately ½ cup)**
>
> **1 avocado, cubed**
>
> **¼ cup Mexicali Sunrise Dressing (page 138), Easy Vinaigrette (page 131), Sun-dried Tomato Herb Dressing (page 137), or Lemon Tahini Dressing (page 133)**
>
> **1 cup kidney beans, precooked, or, if using canned, drained and well rinsed**
>
> **2 tablespoons grated Parmesan (optional)**

Combine lettuce, carrot, and avocado in a big salad bowl. Just before serving, toss with dressing and top with kidney beans and Parmesan cheese.

SEAWEED SALAD

In a rush •• Vegan •• Raw

Seaweeds—or "sea vegetables" as they're also called—are nutrient-rich superfoods packed with trace minerals that are hard to get elsewhere in our diets. For some people they take a little getting used to, but they are delicious and incredibly good for you. You can find seaweed at your local Asian market or health food store. This is an easy and fast way to prepare it. Pair this recipe with Seared Tuna (page 171) and a side of Quinoa (page 54) for a full meal.

Makes 4 servings

½ **cup dried seaweed (try a combination of wakame, arame, dulse, and kelp, or a mixed-seaweed packet)**

4 cups chopped red or green leaf lettuce

1 small carrot, grated (approximately ½ cup)

¼ **cup Speedy Asian Dressing (page 139)**

1 tablespoon sesame seeds

If the pieces of seaweed are large, use scissors to cut them into smaller pieces. Dried seaweed expands significantly in water, so cut them into smaller pieces than you want. Put in a bowl of cold filtered water for 3 to 4 minutes to soften.

Drain seaweed well, and toss in large salad bowl with remaining vegetables and Speedy Asian Dressing. Sprinkle with sesame seeds and serve immediately.

Tip: Chill your serving bowls in the freezer while you prepare the salad. Salads will stay crisp longer in cold dishes.

RAW KALE AND CABBAGE SALAD

In a rush •• Vegan •• Raw

Kale is one of our favorite vegetables, and we're always looking for new and creative ways to eat it. Raw kale is a little tough and can be bitter—adding the acidity of the apple cider vinegar "cooks" the kale, making it more digestible, without any heat or damage to the delicate nutrients and enzymes. Add some leftover chicken, Teriyaki Tempeh (page 178), or sautéed shrimp to make this a full meal.

Makes 2 large servings

- ½ head napa cabbage, stemmed (approximately 4 cups)
- 1 teaspoon sea salt
- 3 tablespoons apple cider vinegar
- 1 small piece of ginger, approximately ½ inch long
- 1 carrot
- 1 cup thinly sliced kale, stemmed
- ½ teaspoon red pepper flakes
- ¼ teaspoon granulated garlic
- 2 tablespoons sesame seeds or ¼ cup crushed raw peanuts (you can substitute 2 tablespoons of peanut butter if you don't have any seeds or nuts)

Thinly slice cabbage and put into a mixing bowl. Sprinkle with sea salt. Add apple cider vinegar and mix well. Grate ginger and carrot right into bowl, and then add kale. Mix well with a spatula, crushing the kale and cabbage as you mix it to initiate the breakdown of the leaves. You can use your hands to really mix everything and continue to crush the leaves.

Sprinkle with red pepper flakes, granulated garlic, and sesame seeds. Serve.

SHAVED BEET ARUGULA SALAD

Everyday •• Vegetarian, with vegan option •• Better than naked

Beets are often used roasted or pickled, but they're also delicious lightly steamed. This salad makes use of some different varieties of beets—golden and candied—which you can find at the farmers market. They're easier to work with than your normal red beets because they don't dye everything red. This recipe is easiest to make if you have a mandoline, but a block grater will also do, as will your veggie peeler. Ideally you want the beets to be as thin as possible.

For a vegan version of this recipe, omit the Gorgonzola cheese.

Makes 4 servings

> **3 golden or candied beets (or a combination of the two)**
>
> **1 packed cup arugula**
>
> **½ cup raw pecans or walnuts, chopped (ideally presoaked and dehydrated or slow-roasted)**
>
> **¼ cup crumbled Gorgonzola cheese (optional)**
>
> **⅓ to ½ cup Honey-less Mustard Dressing (page 146) or Carrot Ginger Dressing (page 149)**

If your beets came with the greens attached, chop off the greens at the base of the stem. (Don't throw these greens away! You can steam them and use them with fish or your morning eggs.) Wash and peel the beets.

Using a mandoline or the single-blade side of your block grater, shave the beets into thin slices. If your beets are large, cut them in half lengthwise before shaving them to make slightly smaller pieces. You want the beets as thin as possible.

Using a steamer basket, steam the shaved beets for 1 to 2 minutes. Set aside to cool for a
couple of minutes. Toss beets with arugula, nuts, and cheese. Divide among four plates,
and drizzle with Honey-less Mustard Dressing.

LONG LIFE GREENS

Everyday •• Vegan •• Better than naked

Most of us could use more green in our diets. This recipe is a delicious and easy way to include a bunch of your favorites. We've paired it with Teriyaki Sauce but you can add any of your favorite sauces from this book. You can also add protein to this dish: shrimp, chicken, beef, or tempeh.

Makes 4 servings

1 teaspoon unrefined coconut oil

4 large shiitake mushrooms, thinly sliced (approximately 1 cup)

4 cloves garlic, cut into thin rounds

2 cups 1-inch-cut green beans

2 cups ½-inch-sliced red Swiss chard, including stem (keep sliced stem separate)

2 cups stringed and thinly cut (on the diagonal) snow peas or sugar snap peas

1 cup almonds, ideally presoaked and dehydrated or slow-roasted, coarsely chopped

½ teaspoon chili flakes (optional)

1 teaspoon thinly sliced scallions, white and green parts

½ cup Teriyaki Sauce (page 152)

Heat coconut oil in a large sauté pan over medium heat. Add shiitake mushrooms and cook until soft, 2 to 3 minutes. Add garlic and continue cooking for 1 to 2 minutes. Add green beans and the stem portion of Swiss chard. Add 1 teaspoon water, cover pan, and lightly steam the vegetables for 1 to 2 minutes. Remove vegetables from heat and set aside in a large bowl. Add snow peas, chard leaves, and almonds, and toss. The residual heat will lightly cook the snow peas and chard leaves.

To serve, plate the veggies and sprinkle with chili flakes and scallions. Then drizzle with Teriyaki Sauce and serve.

ROASTED YAM CHIPS

Everyday •• Vegan

There's a reason potato chips are one of the most popular snack foods. They satisfy all sorts of hankerings at once—they're salty, carby, and crispy. The problem with most potato chips is that they use poor-quality oils at high temperatures, which means the oils are rancid and very inflammatory, and they usually contain way too much salt. Our version switches out the potatoes for yams and the overrefined vegetable oil for coconut oil (ideally suited for high-temperature cooking), and it uses very little salt. These chips are easy to make and very yummy.

Makes four ½-cup servings

> 1 tablespoon unrefined coconut oil
>
> 3 to 4 yams
>
> ½ teaspoon sea salt
>
> 1 teaspoon paprika
>
> 1 teaspoon thyme

Preheat oven to 395°F. While oven is preheating, put coconut oil in a heat-resistant bowl into the oven to melt. As oil is melting and oven is heating, slice yams into thin rounds, about ¼ inch thick.

When oil has melted, remove from the oven and add salt, paprika, and thyme. Add sliced yams and toss until well coated. Lay coated yams in a single layer on an oven tray and place in oven.

Check and flip yams with a flat metal spatula after 10 to 12 minutes. Yams should be crispy with some color after 20 to 25 minutes cooking time. Remove from oven and serve warm. Do *not* leave on hot tray because they will continue to cook and may burn.

GARLICKY HERB RED POTATOES

Everyday •• Vegetarian, with vegan option

This recipe almost didn't make it into the book because it reveals one of James's (formerly) top-secret tricks for roasting potatoes that will have your friends and family oohing and aahing with every bite. While it doesn't take enough time to warrant going in the "impress the neighbors" category, this recipe will certainly impress.

For a vegan version of this recipe, substitute coconut oil for ghee and sesame oil for olive oil.

Makes 8 (½ cup) servings

> 1 tablespoon ghee or unrefined coconut oil
>
> 6 red potatoes, cut into 4 wedges and then halved (about 4 cups)
>
> ¾ teaspoon sea salt
>
> 6 garlic cloves, roasted (see sidebar)
>
> 1 teaspoon extra-virgin olive oil or sesame oil
>
> 1 teaspoon chopped fresh parsley

Put ghee in a heat-resistant bowl and put in the oven, along with the oven tray. Preheat oven to 395°F. While oven is heating, tray is warming, and ghee is melting, prepare the potatoes.

When ghee has melted, remove from the oven. Add potatoes and 2 teaspoon of the salt to the melted ghee in the bowl. Toss until well coated. Lay coated potatoes on the heated oven tray and place in oven. Check and flip potatoes with a flat metal spatula after 10 to 12 minutes. Return to oven and cook for 10 to 12 minutes more, until potatoes are crispy with some color. Remove from oven and place in a bowl while still hot.

While potatoes are cooking, prepare garlic herb mixture: Place roasted garlic and remaining 4 teaspoon of the salt on a cutting board. Using the side of a knife, mash them together into a paste. Scrape the paste into a large bowl and add oil and parsley. Mix well.

Toss the crispy, hot potatoes with the garlic herb paste until well coated. Serve warm.

Roasted Garlic

To roast garlic, preheat oven to 395°F. Place individual cloves in a small heat-resistant ramekin. Add ¼ teaspoon ghee (or unrefined coconut oil for a vegan version) and a pinch of sea salt, and cover the ramekin with aluminum foil. Place covered ramekin in oven until garlic is a nice brown roasted color, about 15 minutes. Store in a sealed container in the fridge. Best if used within 3 days. If you're following the Garlicky Herb Red Potatoes recipe, you can roast the garlic at the same time as you're roasting the potatoes.

OMEGA-RICH ARUGULA SALAD

Everyday •• Pescatarian •• Better than naked

This is a nice and hearty spring salad, with the bitter arugula offset by the salty sardines and goat cheese. Sardines are an excellent source of the omega-3 fatty acids that are so important and so lacking in most people's diets, and because these fish are small and low on the food chain, this means they're typically quite low in PCB (polychlorinated biphenyl) and methylmercury toxicity, which is often a concern when it comes to fish and seafood.

We've added a scoop of Sheree's Green Cultured Vegetables to show how nicely they complement any kind of salad.

Makes 4 servings

2 cups arugula

2½ cups chopped romaine lettuce

½ cup cherry tomatoes, sliced lengthwise

2 (4-ounce) cans of sardines, packed in water, drained and broken into pieces

2 carrots, cut into thin rounds (approximately ½ cup)

1 scallion, finely chopped

½ cup sprouted mung beans (see sprouting instructions on page 32)

½ cup Honey Miso Dressing (page 150)

¼ cup crumbled goat cheese

¼ cup Sheree's Green Cultured Vegetables (page 72)

Prepare vegetables and sardines. Toss arugula, romaine lettuce, tomatoes, sardines, carrots, scallion, and sprouted mung beans in a large salad bowl.

Just before serving, toss vegetables with the dressing. Sprinkle with goat cheese and cultured vegetables, and serve.

SWEET POTATO MASH

Everyday •• Vegan, with vegetarian and omnivore options

This is a great alternative to your standard mashed potatoes, and makes great use of the oven if you're already using it for roasting. We use it as a topping for Sweet Potato Shepherd's Pie (page 198).

For a vegan version of this recipe, blend the potatoes with water; for a vegetarian version, use Kitchen Scraps Veggie Stock; and for an omnivore version, use Beef Bone Broth.

Makes four to six ½-cup servings

  2 tablespoons unrefined coconut oil

  2 pounds sweet potatoes, peeled and cut into 1-inch chunks

  6 garlic cloves, peeled

  ½ to 1 cup water, Kitchen Scraps Veggie Stock (page 50), or Beef Bone Broth (page 49)

  Sea salt

  Freshly ground pepper

Preheat oven to 395°F. If your kitchen is slightly cool and your coconut oil is solid, put it in a large heat-resistant bowl and into the oven to melt. Remove from oven when melted.

Toss sweet potatoes and garlic with the oil to coat thoroughly, and spread out on oven tray. Bake for 15 minutes, until soft.

Put the cooked potatoes, garlic, and ½ cup of water or stock in your blender. Blend to the desired consistency. You may need to add more water or stock. Season with sea salt and freshly ground pepper to taste.

ROASTED CAULIFLOWER MASH

Everyday •• Vegetarian, with vegan option

Watching your starchy carbohydrate intake but love your mashed potatoes? This is the recipe for you. Mashing roasted cauliflower is one of the many ways we use cauliflower to mimic less-nutritious comfort foods. For a vegan version of this recipe, simply substitute coconut oil for ghee and use water instead of Kitchen Scraps Veggie Stock.

Makes 4 servings

> 1 tablespoon ghee, butter, or unrefined coconut oil
>
> 1 head cauliflower, stemmed and coarsely chopped
>
> 3 cloves garlic, peeled
>
> ⅛ teaspoon sea salt
>
> ¼ teaspoon paprika
>
> ¼ to ½ cup Kitchen Scraps Veggie Stock (page 50) or water

Preheat oven to 375°F. If your kitchen is cool and the ghee is solid, put it in a large heat-resistant mixing bowl and into the preheating oven to melt. Remove from oven when melted.

Toss cauliflower and garlic cloves with ghee, sea salt, and paprika to coat.

Spread mixture out on an oven tray and roast for 10 to 15 minutes, until cooked through and slightly browned. Remove from oven and put in the food processor or blender, along with stock, and pulse until it is the consistency of mashed potatoes. You might need to add a little more stock, depending on how creamy you like them.

Serve as you would mashed potatoes, or use as an alternate topping for Sweet Potato Shepherd's Pie (page 198).

ROASTED ASPARAGUS

Everyday •• Vegetarian, with vegan option

Roasting asparagus is a healthier alternative to grilling it. You get a little of that nice browning, but not as many of the toxins that you get from the barbecue smoke. This recipe is ultrasimple and easy to do, and complements any fish or meat dish nicely.

For a vegan version of this recipe, substitute coconut oil for ghee.

Makes 2 to 4 servings

1 bunch asparagus spears

1 tablespoon ghee or unrefined coconut oil

Sea salt

Freshly ground pepper

Preheat oven to 395°F. If the ghee is solid, put it in a heat-resistant bowl and into the preheating oven so it can melt.

Wash asparagus spears and chop off ends. Toss them in melted ghee with a little salt and pepper to taste.

Spread asparagus out on an oven tray in a single layer and roast for 12 to 15 minutes, until bright green with a little browning. Be careful not to overcook. Serve warm.

ROASTED BRUSSELS SPROUTS

Everyday •• Vegetarian, with vegan option

Brussels sprouts are one of those vegetables that can make people's toes curl under. Often they're smothered in sugar to make them palatable, but that's not such a naked solution. This recipe is a simple way to make them taste delicious and turn even the most reluctant Brussels sprouts eater into a fan.

For a vegan version of this recipe, substitute coconut oil for butter.

Makes 4 servings

1 to 2 tablespoons ghee or unrefined coconut oil

1 stem Brussels sprouts (approximately 20 sprouts)

Sea salt

Freshly ground pepper

Preheat oven to 385°F.

Put ghee (if solid) into a heat-resistant bowl and then into the preheating oven to melt. Chop the Brussels sprouts off the stem and cut them in half lengthwise. When ghee has melted, pull bowl out of oven, add Brussels sprouts, and toss with salt and pepper to taste.

Spread the Brussels sprouts out on an oven tray in a single layer. Roast for about 20 minutes, until lightly browned, turning occasionally to make sure they cook on all sides. Serve warm.

ASIAN FUSION SALAD

Everyday •• Vegan •• Better than naked

Some version of this salad is regularly featured at our house. We love Asian salads, but we don't like the fried noodle bits and oversweet canned mandarin oranges that typically come with them. This is our naked version without those overprocessed ingredients. You can find the mung bean noodles, arame seaweed, and daikon radish at your local Asian market or health food store.

Makes 2 servings

½ cup mung bean noodles (also known as glass noodles)

2 tablespoons arame seaweed

2 cups shredded napa cabbage

1 cup baby spinach

½ cup grated daikon radish

½ cup grated carrot

6 to 8 snow peas, cut into thin diagonal slices (approximately ½ cup)

2 tablespoons 1-inch-long thin slices red bell pepper

¼ cup thinly sliced (into half moons) Persian cucumber

¼ cup Carrot Ginger Dressing (page 149), Speedy Asian Dressing (page 139), or Lemon Tahini Dressing (page 133)

2 tablespoons crushed cashews, preferably presoaked and dehydrated or slow-roasted

2 teaspoons thinly sliced green onions, green parts only

¼ cup Crispy Shiitake Faux Bacon (page 57) (optional)

In a small saucepan, bring 2 cups water to a boil. Add mung bean noodles, turn off the heat, and let noodles sit in hot water for 10 minutes while you are preparing the rest of the vegetables. In a small bowl, cover arame seaweed with cold filtered water and set aside to soak while you're preparing the other ingredients.

Prepare cabbage, spinach, daikon radish, carrot, snow peas, bell pepper, and cucumber, and combine in a large salad bowl. Remove arame seaweed from water, rinse and drain well, and then add to the bowl. Pour mung bean noodles into a colander and run under cold water to cool. Drain well and add to the bowl.

Just before serving, toss vegetables with the salad dressing. Sprinkle with cashews, green onions, and shiitake mushrooms.

WILD RICE SALAD

Everyday •• Vegetarian, with vegan option •• Better than naked

This salad can be paired with any of the following dressings: Creamy Mint Magic (page 136), Vegan Caesar (Page 145), Light Lemon Flax (page 140), or Honey-less Mustard (page 146).

Look for a wild and whole-grain brown rice blend. Many different companies make these mixes; what you're looking for is a mix that uses only whole, unrefined rices, such as long-grain brown rice, wild rice, and sweet brown rice. For the raisins, use any unsweetened raisin. Our favorite is the golden hunza.

For a vegan version of this recipe, omit the goat cheese.

Makes 3 servings

 1½ cups presoaked, cooked, and chilled mixed wild rice

 ½ cup unsweetened raisins or cut-up dried apricots

 2 cups chopped spinach

 1 cup chopped arugula

 ½ cup crumbled pecans, preferably soaked and dehydrated or slow-roasted

 ½ cup cherry tomatoes, quartered

 ½ cup grated red radish

 ½ cup goat cheese (can be feta or chèvre)

 ¼ cup dressing of your choice (see suggestions above)

Combine all ingredients in a large mixing bowl and toss to mix well. Either eat immediately or chill until ready to serve. To enhance the flavors, let the salad sit for 1 or more hours.

CHILI CHEESE FRIES

Everyday •• Vegetarian, with omnivore option

The title alone inspires guilt, but this recipe has nothing in it for you to feel bad about. This is a great example of a naked version of a comfort-food favorite.

For the omnivore version of this recipe, use lard instead of ghee.

Makes 4 servings

> **1 tablespoon ghee or lard**
>
> **3 to 4 cups fingerling potatoes, red or white, or a combination**
>
> **1 teaspoon chili powder**
>
> **½ teaspoon oregano**
>
> **½ teaspoon granulated garlic**
>
> **½ teaspoon sea salt**
>
> **½ cup grated aged cheddar cheese**

Preheat oven to 400°F. Put an oven tray into the oven as it preheats so that it's nice and hot when it comes time to put the potatoes on it. Put ghee in a heat-resistant bowl and into the oven as well to melt.

While ghee and oven are heating, cut fingerling potatoes lengthwise into wedges. Mix together chili powder, oregano, garlic, and sea salt in a small bowl.

When ghee has melted, toss potatoes, seasonings, and ghee together in the heated bowl, coating potatoes well. Spread potatoes out on the heated oven tray and bake for 15 minutes. Remove from oven and turn the potatoes using a metal spatula. Sprinkle with the cheddar cheese and put back into the oven for another 10 minutes. Use a metal spatula to remove potatoes from tray and serve warm.

Tip: If you're doubling the recipe and can't cook all of the potatoes at the same time, keep the uncooked cut potatoes in a bowl of cold water while you're cooking the first batch. This is an easy trick to keep them from turning brown.

QUINOA TABOULEH

Everyday •• Vegan, with pescatarian option •• Better than naked

This recipe makes use of soaked and toasted quinoa, which is tremendously light, fluffy, and nutty. It's a gluten-free alternative to the dish normally made with bulgur wheat. We've included an optional addition of sardines or anchovies, to make it a complete meal. Or it makes a nice side dish to complement just about any protein.

For a pescatarian version of this recipe, add sardines or anchovies.

Makes 3 to 4 servings

> **1 recipe Quinoa (page 54)**
>
> **1 small cucumber, diced (approximately 1 cup)**
>
> **1 carrot, grated (approximately 1 cup)**
>
> **½ cup quartered cherry tomatoes**
>
> **½ cup chopped fresh parsley**
>
> **¼ cup chopped fresh mint**
>
> **2 tablespoons lemon juice**
>
> **3 tablespoons extra-virgin olive oil**
>
> **1 tablespoon minced scallion**
>
> **¼ teaspoon paprika**
>
> **¼ to ½ teaspoon sea salt**
>
> **1 small can sardines or anchovies (optional)**

Follow the recipe for Quinoa. While the Quinoa is cooking, prepare the vegetables. When the Quinoa has been fully cooked, let cool, and then toss with the vegetables, lemon juice, olive oil, scallion, paprika, and sea salt to taste. Drain the sardines or anchovies, chop them roughly, and toss with the tabouleh. Store in the refrigerator or eat immediately.

ROASTED JERUSALEM ARTICHOKES

Everyday •• Vegetarian, with vegan option

Jerusalem artichokes are one of those root vegetables you'll find in the spring at the farmers market that most people have no idea how to prepare. Much more common in Europe than in North America, Jerusalem artichokes are a great alternative to potatoes. They have a much lower glycemic load yet they still have that starchy feel. They taste kind of like a combination of potato and artichoke. Very different from the artichokes we're all used to, Jerusalem artichokes look a lot like bulbous ginger. For a vegan option, substitute coconut oil for ghee.

Makes 3 to 4 servings

> **2 tablespoons ghee or unrefined coconut oil**
>
> **2 cups 1-inch pieces Jerusalem artichokes**
>
> **½ teaspoon sea salt**
>
> **¼ teaspoon freshly ground pepper**

Preheat oven to 375°F. While the oven is preheating, put the ghee in a heat-resistant bowl and into the oven to melt.

When the ghee has melted, remove it from the oven and add the artichokes, sea salt, and pepper. Toss to coat the artichokes well. Spread them out on an oven tray and bake for 10 minutes. Remove from heat and turn using a metal spatula. Put back in the oven for another 10 minutes. Using the same spatula, remove from tray and serve warm.

SHAVED FENNEL, PEAR, AND GORGONZOLA SALAD

Everyday •• Vegetarian, with vegan option

This is a really refreshing salad, ideal on a spring or summer day. For a vegan version of this salad, substitute avocado for Gorgonzola.

Makes 4 servings

1 large bulb fennel

1 small pear

½ small cucumber

Zest and juice of 1 lime

2 tablespoons flaxseed oil

Sea salt

Freshly ground pepper

4 cups mixed greens

¼ cup crumbled Gorgonzola cheese or finely diced avocado

Remove the top of the fennel and cut off the green, feathery fronds. Set the fronds aside to use as a garnish later on, discarding the rest of the fennel top. Trim the bulb ends and cut bulb in half lengthwise. Using a mandoline or a very sharp knife, cut bulb halves into very thin slices. Put in a large mixing bowl and set aside.

Wash and core pear, then cut into very thin slices. You can use a vegetable peeler to make the slices particularly thin. Cut the cucumber into very thin half moons. Add the pear and cucumber slices to the fennel.

In a small bowl, combine zest and juice of one lime, flaxseed oil, and salt and pepper to taste. Using a whisk, mix well. Toss dressing with fennel, pear, and cucumber, coating the fruit and vegetables well.

To plate, put 1 cup of mixed greens on each plate, topped with one-fourth of the fennel mixture. Sprinkle with Gorgonzola cheese and a teaspoon of minced fennel fronds, and serve.

SAVORY SWEET POTATO PANCAKES

Everyday •• Vegetarian, with vegan option

These pancakes are very versatile. You can have them as a side for your dinner, use them for a fancy breakfast, or even create mini-pancakes as appetizers. This recipe uses arrowroot instead of flour to keep the pancakes gluten-free. Substitute coconut oil for ghee for a vegan option. You can find arrowroot in the spice section of most grocery stores, or buy in bulk at one of the specialty stores we included in the "Resources" section at www.eatnakednow.com.

Makes 8 (3-inch) pancakes

> 1 sweet potato, grated (approximately 1 cup)
>
> 1 zucchini, grated (approximately 1 cup)
>
> 2 tablespoons minced parsley
>
> 1 tablespoon minced green onion, green parts only
>
> ½ bunch kale, stemmed and finely chopped (approximately 1 cup)
>
> 2 eggs
>
> 1 tablespoon arrowroot
>
> ½ teaspoon sea salt
>
> ½ teaspoon paprika
>
> ¼ teaspoon freshly ground pepper
>
> ½ to 1 tablespoon ghee or unrefined coconut oil

In a large mixing bowl, combine sweet potato, zucchini, parsley, green onion, and kale. In a separate small bowl, mix eggs, arrowroot, sea salt, paprika, and pepper. Add egg mixture to sweet potato and other vegetables, and mix well.

In a large skillet, heat ½ tablespoon ghee over medium heat. When pan is hot, scoop up ¼ cup of potato mixture and drop into pan to form a pancake. Flatten into pancake shape about ¼ inch thick. Repeat for 3 to 4 pancakes, or however many will fit easily into your skillet. Cook for 5 minutes each side, until slightly browned and firm.

After cooking the first batch, remove from heat using a metal spatula and set aside on a rack while you cook the next batches. You want to use a rack rather than a plate so that the pancakes aren't sitting in their own juices. This keeps them nice and crispy. If you want to make sure they stay warm, put the rack on an oven tray and into a warmed oven while you cook the other pancakes. As you're cooking the pancakes, you may need to add more ghee to the pan to keep them from sticking.

CAESAR SALAD

Impress the neighbors •• Vegetarian, with pescatarian and vegan options

This recipe includes both pescatarian and vegan versions on the classic. For those who are pescatarians, we recommend adding Smelt Fry to the salad. For vegans, we recommend Crispy Shiitake Faux Bacon and Vegan Caesar Dressing rather than the usual egg-based Caesar Salad Dressing. To avoid the gluten issue involved with croutons, you use crumbled Zesty Crackers. This is a great way to use the leftover bits and pieces from the cracker recipe.

Makes 4 servings

1 large head romaine lettuce

½ **cup Caesar Salad Dressing (page 144) or Vegan Caesar Dressing (page 145)**

1 recipe Crispy Shiitake Faux Bacon (page 57) or Smelt Fry (page 179)

½ **cup crumbled Zesty Crackers (page 222)**

½ **cup pumpkin seeds, preferably presoaked and dehydrated or slow-roasted**

Chop lettuce into bite-size pieces and put in a large salad bowl. Just before serving, toss lettuce with dressing, and top with either Crispy Shiitake Faux Bacon or Smelt Fry. Sprinkle with Zesty Crackers and pumpkin seeds, and serve immediately.

MEXICAN SALAD

Impress the neighbors •• Vegetarian, with vegan option

The flavors in Mexican food are to die for, but often the meals are high in starch and unhealthy fats. In this recipe, we're taking advantage of the Mexican flavors, but adding all sorts of veggies, taking out the excessive starch and unhealthy fats, and lightening up the feel of the meal overall. Satisfy your hankering for Mexican without all the grease that it usually entails.

For a vegan version of this salad, use coconut oil instead of ghee and omit the cheese.

Makes 4 servings

- **1 teaspoon ghee or unrefined coconut oil**
- **2 corn tortillas, cut into ½-inch strips (approximately ½ heaping cup)**
- **2 cups shredded red cabbage**
- **2½ cups chopped romaine lettuce or spinach**
- **2 radishes, finely chopped or grated**
- **½ cup finely diced tomato**
- **1 to 2 small yellow crooked-neck squash, grated (approximately 1 cup)**
- **1 cup kidney beans, presoaked and cooked (if canned, find a low-sodium variety and drain and rinse well)**
- **½ cup Tomatillo Avocado Sauce (page 148)**
- **2 tablespoons grated cheddar cheese**
- **1 tablespoon pumpkin seeds, preferably presoaked and dehydrated or slow-roasted**

Preheat oven to 375°F. Put the ghee in a heat-resistant bowl and then into the oven, and let it melt. When ghee has melted, toss it with the tortilla strips. Spread out on an oven tray and bake for 10 to 12 minutes, until crispy. Remove and let cool.

While tortilla strips are baking, prepare the cabbage, lettuce, radishes, tomato, and squash. Put in a large salad bowl and toss the vegetables with the kidney beans to mix.

Just before serving, toss with Tomatillo Avocado Sauce and sprinkle with cheese, pumpkin seeds, and tortilla crisps.

LEMON BUTTER ARTICHOKES

Impress the neighbors •• Vegetarian, with vegan option

Fresh artichokes are such a great way to impress the neighbors, with very little effort. We've included them in the "impress the neighbors" category because they take up to an hour to cook, but most of that time is unattended. They make a delicious first course or complement to any meal in summer, when they're in season.

For a vegan version of this recipe, substitute extra-virgin olive oil for butter.

Makes 2 servings

>   **2 artichokes**
>
>   **2 cloves garlic, peeled**
>
>   **1 bay leaf**
>
>   **½ tablespoon lemon juice, saving the rind**
>
>   **1 tablespoon butter or extra-virgin olive oil**
>
>   **Sea salt**
>
>   **Freshly ground pepper**

Chop off bottom of artichoke stems, and discard any small or discolored leaves at base of flower. Put the artichokes, garlic, bay leaf, and the rind from the already-juiced lemon in a large saucepan filled halfway with water. Cover, bring the water to a boil, and then cook, still boiling, for 45 to 60 minutes (time will depend on how large the artichokes are). The artichoke is cooked when a sharp knife easily goes through the base of the artichoke.

During the last 5 minutes of the artichokes' cooking time, combine the butter, lemon juice, and salt and pepper to taste into a small pan, and heat on low until butter has just melted. Set aside.

When artichokes have finished cooking, remove them from the water with tongs, let any water still in them drain out, and put them in serving bowls. Let cool for 5 minutes.

Serve with the lemon butter as a dipping sauce. Eating an artichoke is an art unto itself. For a video demonstration, search "artichoke" on www.eatnakednow.com/videos.

RAW CAULIFLOWER "COUSCOUS" GREEK SALAD

Impress the neighbors •• Vegetarian, with vegan option

This is a raw, gluten-free twist on a couple of classics: Mediterranean couscous and a Greek salad. It's an excellent party recipe and provides its own party game: having people guess the "secret" ingredient that makes up the "couscous." So far we've never had anyone guess it!

For a vegan version of this salad, simply omit the cheese.

Makes 4 servings

1 head cauliflower

½ cup firmly packed fresh basil

¼ cup firmly packed fresh mint

1 cup firmly packed fresh parsley

1 small clove garlic

1 English cucumber, cubed (approximately 2 cups)

1 red bell pepper, cubed (approximately 1 cup)

½ cup julienned sun-dried tomatoes

Juice of 1 lemon (approximately ¼ cup)

½ cup extra-virgin olive oil

½ teaspoon sea salt

¼ teaspoon freshly ground black pepper

¼ teaspoon paprika

¼ teaspoon ground cumin

2 heads romaine lettuce, chopped (approximately 8 cups)

½ cup pitted and halved kalamata olives

½ cup pine nuts

1 cup crumbled feta cheese (we prefer goat or sheep's feta, but cow's feta will work too)

A few thin slices of red onion

Break the cauliflower into big chunks and put in a food processor along with basil, mint, parsley, and garlic. Pulse several times until minced. The cauliflower will have a granular consistency—much like couscous. You might have to do this in several batches depending on the size of your food processor. Set the cauliflower mixture aside in a big bowl.

Add cucumber, bell pepper, and sun-dried tomatoes to the cauliflower.

In a small bowl, whisk together lemon juice, olive oil, salt, black pepper, paprika, and cumin. Toss this dressing with the cauliflower mixture thoroughly.

Put the lettuce in a big salad bowl. Top with the cauliflower mixture just before serving and mix thoroughly. (Note: The lettuce will wilt once you put the dressing on it, so don't toss until you're just about to eat it.) Sprinkle with olives, pine nuts, feta cheese, and red onion, and serve immediately.

Note about sun-dried tomatoes: We prefer to get our sun-dried tomatoes dry, not packed in any oil. If your sun-dried tomatoes are extremely hard, you'll need to reconstitute them by soaking them in warm water for 10 to 15 minutes. If they're a little soft and chewy, you can use them as is, without reconstituting.

MEDITERRANEAN LENTIL SALAD

Impress the neighbors •• Vegetarian, with vegan option

This is a nutrient-packed vegetarian salad and can stand alone as a full meal. The French lentils, when cooked, are firmer and slightly smaller than other lentils. This recipe also uses sumac, a Middle Eastern spice with a tart, lemony flavor. You can find it at your local Middle Eastern market or health food store. If you have trouble finding it, simply omit it. See the "Resources" page at www.eatnakednow.com for sources.

For a vegan version of this salad, substitute coconut oil for ghee.

Makes 4 servings

2 cups French Lentils (page 46)

2 teaspoons ghee or unrefined coconut oil

1 onion, sliced thinly lengthwise (approximately 1 cup)

½ teaspoon sea salt

1 cup cherry tomatoes, quartered

½ cup grated carrot

1 cucumber, peeled and cut into ¼-inch dice (approximately 1 cup)

2 tablespoons thinly sliced scallions

2 cups chopped spinach

½ cup chopped parsley

Zest of 1 lemon

Juice of 2 lemons

½ teaspoon freshly ground pepper

1 tablespoon sumac (optional)

¼ cup extra-virgin olive oil

If you have not already cooked the lentils, prepare them as described in the recipe. As the lentils are cooking, heat ghee in a large skillet over medium heat. Sauté the onions with salt over low heat until caramelized—they'll develop a brownish hue and will sweeten slightly. This takes 15 to 20 minutes.

When lentils have cooked, drain any remaining water, and let cool by spreading them out on an oven tray. When cool, combine lentils with tomatoes, carrot, cucumber, scallions, spinach, parsley, and lemon zest in a large salad bowl. Toss to mix well.

To make the dressing: Combine caramelized onions, lemon juice, pepper, and sumac in a blender and blend until smooth. With blender still running, slowly pour in olive oil and continue blending until smooth. Toss the salad with the dressing immediately before serving.

9
Sauces, Dressings, and Dips

As we mentioned of condiments in the "Basics" chapter, a lot of un-naked ingredients hide in commercially available sauces, dressings, and dips. Even "healthy" salad dressings use very low-quality refined vegetable oils that are rancid before you've even opened the bottle. Most oils used in commercial salad dressings are polyunsaturated oils that are highly unstable and go rancid easily. The processing of them alone will damage them, but unlike other nutrients, a lot of oils don't smell when they've gone rancid, so it's difficult to tell by flavor alone. We recommend that you just make your own rather than play a guessing game. Also, the number of preservatives, flavorings, colorings, and emulsifiers in store-bought dressings is dizzying.

We've purposely kept these recipes simple. We find the biggest hurdle people have with making their own dressings or sauces is the misperception that it's time consuming. To sway even the most hardened and busy person, we've included a whole series of dressings in the "in a rush" category that simply use a mason jar and some good shaking.

With only a few exceptions, the recipes in this chapter are in the category of "make it once, use it lots." We highly recommend that you take some time on the weekend to make one or two dressings each week, and then use them throughout the week. It will reduce the prep time of your other meals significantly. All it takes is a little planning. For help and ideas, see Appendix A, "One-Week Naked Menus."

Most of these recipes are vegetarian or vegan but can be used with vegetables, meat, or fish.

EASY VINAIGRETTE

In a rush •• Vegan •• Make it once, use it lots

If you're in a rush but want to use your own dressing rather than store-bought (something we highly recommend, since almost all store-bought dressings—even the "healthy" ones— use poor-quality oils), here's a basic oil and vinegar dressing you can make in minutes. Try experimenting with different oils such as hemp seed oil, pumpkin seed oil, and flaxseed oil, and different vinegars such as apple cider vinegar and red wine vinegar.

We use this dressing with Speedy Green Salad (page 103).

Makes 1 cup

¾ cup extra-virgin olive oil (or hemp seed, pumpkin seed, or flax oil)

¼ cup high-quality balsamic vinegar (or apple cider or red wine vinegar)

Pinch sea salt

Freshly ground pepper

Combine all ingredients in a glass jar. Place lid on top, seal tightly, and shake vigorously. Enjoy over greens.

Store in the refrigerator for up to 1 week, but remember that olive oil solidifies in the fridge due to its high monounsaturated fatty-acid content. You'll need to leave it at room temperature for a few minutes after you've taken it out of the fridge. Shake well before using.

GREEN GODDESS DIP

In a rush •• Vegan •• Make it once, use it lots

This dip is excellent with Zesty Crackers (page 222) or Sea Crackers (page 224). Or serve it with a plate of raw veggies instead of the overused hummus. This recipe uses tahini, which is a paste made from sesame seeds. Look for brands made with raw sesame seeds and without any added salt or other ingredients.

Makes 1 cup

½ packed cup cilantro

1 jalapeño pepper, stemmed and seeded

2 tablespoons tahini

2 cloves garlic, peeled

Juice of 2 limes (approximately 2 tablespoons)

½ teaspoon sea salt

½ avocado, flesh scooped out

1 tablespoon extra-virgin olive oil

Combine all ingredients in a blender, add ½ cup filtered water, and blend until smooth. Use immediately or store in the refrigerator in a glass container for up to 4 days. Shake well before using.

Note: Because this dressing uses olive oil, it will solidify when you put it in the fridge. Remember to let it sit at room temperature for 10 to 15 minutes before use.

LEMON TAHINI DRESSING

In a rush •• Vegan •• Make it once, use it lots

This is a nice, light dressing you can use with just about any salad. It's a little like a very light and liquid hummus. We use it with Speedy Green Salad (page 103) and Asian Fusion Salad (page 116). This recipe uses tahini, which is a paste made from sesame seeds. Look for brands made with raw sesame seeds and without any added salt or other ingredients.

Makes 1 cup

- ¼ cup lemon juice
- 1 rounded tablespoon tahini
- 1 clove garlic, peeled
- ½ teaspoon sea salt
- ⅛ teaspoon ground cumin
- ⅛ teaspoon freshly ground pepper
- ¾ cup extra-virgin olive oil

Combine lemon juice, tahini, garlic clove, sea salt, cumin, and pepper in blender. Purée until smooth. With blender still running, slowly drizzle in olive oil and continue to blend until smooth. Store in fridge for up to 1 week.

Note: Because this dressing uses olive oil, it will solidify when you put it in the fridge. Remember to let it sit at room temperature for 10 to 15 minutes before use.

SPEEDY PEANUT DRESSING

In a rush •• Vegan •• Make it once, use it lots

As with our other dressings and sauces, this recipe makes a large batch that you can store in the fridge and use repeatedly. This uses our cook naked principle of leveraging the time spent in the kitchen: Make it once, use it several times. This dressing has a nice Asian hint to it. Pair it with Asian Fusion Salad (page 116) or any Asian-style dish.

Makes approximately 1 cup

> ¾ **cup peanut oil**
>
> **Juice of 1 lime (approximately 2 tablespoons plus 1 teaspoon)**
>
> **2 tablespoons peanut butter**
>
> **1 tablespoon gluten-free tamari soy sauce**

Combine all ingredients in a pint-size mason jar. Cover with lid and shake well. Use immediately or refrigerate for up to 2 weeks until ready to use. Shake well before using.

Tip: To optimize the amount of juice you can get from a lime or lemon, roll it on a board before cutting it, applying pressure with your hand. This softens the lime, and you'll be able to squeeze more juice out of it.

Note: Because this dressing uses peanut oil, it will solidify when you put it in the fridge. Remember to let it sit at room temperature for 10 to 15 minutes before use.

IN A HURRY CURRY DRESSING

In a rush •• Vegetarian •• Make it once, use it lots

This dressing pairs nicely with any Indian-style dish—it's also a really easy way to add a curry flavor to anything. We use it in the recipe for Curried Swiss Chard with Almonds (page 102).

Makes a little more than ½ cup

½ cup store-bought or homemade Yogurt (page 65)

1 tablespoon lemon juice

1 teaspoon raw honey

½ teaspoon curry powder

½ teaspoon thyme

½ teaspoon ground cumin

½ teaspoon sea salt

Combine all ingredients in a pint-size mason jar. Shake vigorously to mix. Either use immediately or store in the refrigerator until ready to use. Keeps for up to 1 week. Shake well before using.

CREAMY MINT MAGIC DRESSING

In a rush •• Vegan •• Make it once, use it lots

As with our other dressings and sauces, this recipe makes a large batch that you can store in the fridge and use repeatedly. This uses our cook naked principle of leveraging the time spent in the kitchen: Make it once, use it several times. It's a nice, refreshing summertime dressing. Because it's a little sour, it goes particularly well with sweet summer salads, like Melon Cucumber Salad (page 99).

Makes 1 heaping cup

   1 cup store-bought or homemade Coconut Milk (page 44)

   1 teaspoon raw honey

   1 teaspoon gluten-free tamari soy sauce

   Juice of 1 lime (approximately 2 tablespoons)

   2 tablespoons fresh mint, roughly torn into pieces

Combine all ingredients in a pint-size mason jar. Shake vigorously to mix. Either use immediately or store in the refrigerator until ready to use. Keeps for up to 1 week. Shake well before using.

Note: Because this dressing uses coconut milk, it may solidify when you put it in the fridge. Remember to let it sit at room temperature for 10 to 15 minutes before use.

SUN-DRIED TOMATO HERB DRESSING

In a rush •• Vegan •• Make it once, use it lots

As with our other dressings and sauces, this recipe makes a large batch that you can store in the fridge and use repeatedly. This uses our cook naked principle of leveraging the time spent in the kitchen: Make it once, use it several times. This dressing goes well with any green salad. We use it with Speedy Green Salad (page 103).

Makes 1 to 1½ cups

- 1 cup extra-virgin olive oil
- 2 tablespoons julienned sun-dried tomatoes (use plain sun-dried tomatoes, not those packed in oil)
- Juice of 1 lemon (approximately ¼ cup)
- 2 tablespoons balsamic vinegar
- 1 teaspoon thyme
- 1 teaspoon oregano
- ½ teaspoon sea salt
- Pinch freshly ground pepper

Combine all ingredients in a pint-size mason jar. Shake vigorously to mix. Either use immediately or store in the refrigerator until ready to use. The longer it sits, the more flavorful it will get. Keeps for up to 2 weeks. Shake well before using.

Note: Because this dressing uses olive oil, it will solidify when you put it in the fridge. Remember to let it sit at room temperature for 10 to 15 minutes before use.

Note about sun-dried tomatoes: We prefer to get our sun-dried tomatoes dry, not packed in any oil. If your sun-dried tomatoes are extremely hard, you'll need to reconstitute them by soaking them in warm water for 10 to 15 minutes. If they're a little soft and chewy, you can use them as is, without reconstituting.

MEXICALI SUNRISE DRESSING

In a rush •• Vegan •• Make it once, use it lots

As with our other dressings and sauces, this recipe makes a large batch that you can store in the fridge and use repeatedly. This uses our cook naked principle of leveraging the time spent in the kitchen: Make it once, use it several times. This dressing goes well with any Mexican-style salad. We use it with our Speedy Green Salad (page 103).

Makes 1½ cups

2 Roma tomatoes

2 packed tablespoons cilantro

Juice of 2 limes (approximately ¼ cup)

1 cup extra-virgin olive oil

1 teaspoon thyme

½ teaspoon ground cumin

1 teaspoon chili powder

½ teaspoon granulated garlic

½ teaspoon sea salt

Cut Roma tomatoes in half crosswise, and squeeze out and discard the seeds and extra juices. Combine the cilantro with the remaining tomato flesh, and dice together as small as possible. Don't worry about being precise.

Put tomato and cilantro in a pint-size mason jar and add the remaining ingredients. Shake vigorously to mix. Either use immediately or store in the refrigerator until ready to use. The longer it sits, the more flavorful it will get. Keeps for up to 1 week. Shake well before using.

Note: Because this dressing uses olive oil, it will solidify when you put it in the fridge. Remember to let it sit at room temperature for 10 to 15 minutes to warm up before use.

SPEEDY ASIAN DRESSING

In a rush •• Vegan •• Make it once, use it lots

As with our other dressings and sauces, this recipe makes a large batch that you can store in the fridge and use repeatedly. This uses our cook naked principle of leveraging the time in the kitchen: Make it once, use it several times. This is a light dressing that goes well with any Asian-style dish. We use it with Asian Fusion Salad (page 116) and Seaweed Salad (page 104).

Makes ¾ cup

> ½ **cup raw, unrefined sesame oil**
>
> ½ **teaspoon toasted sesame oil (if you can find hot pepper toasted sesame oil this adds a nice kick)**
>
> 3 **tablespoons gluten-free tamari soy sauce**
>
> **Juice of** ½ **lime (approximately 1 tablespoon)**
>
> 1 **teaspoon grated ginger**
>
> 1 **teaspoon sesame seeds**
>
> **Few sprigs cilantro (6 to 8 leaves, hand shredded)**

Combine all ingredients in a pint-size mason jar. Shake vigorously to mix. Either use immediately or store in the refrigerator until ready to use. The longer it sits, the more flavorful it will get. Keeps for up to 1 week. Shake well before using.

LIGHT LEMON FLAX DRESSING

In a rush •• Vegan •• Make it once, use it lots

This is a recipe Margaret conceived when she was on a very strict elimination diet and wanted an easy and flavorful recipe that had none of the offending substances (sugar, vinegars, or anything processed). As with our other dressings and sauces, this recipe makes a large batch that you can store in the fridge and use repeatedly. This uses our cook naked principle of leveraging the time spent in the kitchen: Make it once, use it several times. Use with any green salad.

Makes 1 cup

> **1 teaspoon whole yellow mustard seed**
>
> **½ teaspoon whole coriander seed**
>
> **1 cup flaxseed oil**
>
> **Juice of 1 lemon (approximately ¼ cup)**
>
> **¼ teaspoon sea salt**
>
> **⅛ teaspoon freshly ground pepper**

Crush the mustard seed and coriander seed using either a dedicated coffee grinder or a mortar and pestle. Combine with other ingredients in a half-pint mason jar, close the lid tightly, and shake vigorously to mix well.

Either use immediately or store in the refrigerator until ready to use. The longer it sits, the more flavorful it will get. Keeps for up to 1 week. Shake well before using.

MEDITERRANEAN PARTY DIP

In a rush •• Vegetarian •• Make it once, use it lots

This recipe makes use of the Cultured Cream Cheese that's a by-product of making Whey. It's fast, easy, and a great naked alternative to store-bought dips that have so many artificial flavorings and preservatives. It's cultured, so it will last you a while if you don't use it immediately.

Makes 1 cup

> 1 cup Cultured Cream Cheese (page 63)
>
> ¼ cup chopped sun-dried tomatoes
>
> 1 tablespoon chives, minced
>
> 1 teaspoon lemon zest
>
> ½ teaspoon sea salt

Combine all ingredients in a mixing bowl and mix well using a spatula. Either use immediately or store in the refrigerator in a glass jar for up to 2 weeks.

Note about sun-dried tomatoes: We prefer to get our sun-dried tomatoes dry, not packed in any oil. If your sun-dried tomatoes are extremely hard, you'll need to reconstitute them by soaking them in warm water for 10 to 15 minutes. If they're a little soft and chewy, you can use them as is, without reconstituting.

MARINARA SAUCE

In a rush •• Vegetarian •• Make it once, use it lots

Marinara is one of the most basic sauces good for any type of meat, vegetable, or grain dish. So versatile and so delicious. We sometimes use it instead of pesto in Pesto Vegetable Linguine (page 190). We also use it on Noodle-less Lasagna (page 192) and Salami Pizza (page 186). This recipe uses both olive oil and butter. Adding the butter protects the olive oil, which is more delicate and breaks down at high temperatures. This is a good trick for when you want the olive oil for the flavor and a stable fat to withstand the heat.

Makes 3½ cups

> 1 tablespoon extra-virgin olive oil
>
> 1 teaspoon butter
>
> 1 small onion, coarsely chopped (approximately 1 cup)
>
> ½ teaspoon sea salt
>
> 1 (28-ounce) can of tomatoes (diced, crushed, or whole), drained
>
> ¼ packed cup fresh basil
>
> 2 tablespoons tomato paste
>
> 1 tablespoon balsamic vinegar

Heat olive oil and butter in a large skillet over medium-low heat. Sauté onion, adding sea salt, for 2 to 3 minutes, until just translucent. Remove from heat.

Put cooked onions in a blender along with tomatoes, basil, tomato paste, and balsamic vinegar. Pulse the blender to purée the sauce.

Make sure the sauce has fully cooled prior to storing in a sealed container in the fridge. Will store for up to 1 week. When ready to use, transfer to small saucepan and heat over medium heat.

UMEBOSHI DRESSING

Everyday •• Vegan •• Better than naked •• Make it once, use it lots

Umeboshi is a naturally fermented (yes, better than naked) paste made from the Japanese ume plum. It has been touted for its many health benefits including easing digestive distress, alkalinizing the body, and supporting the liver. This dressing is delicious paired with fish and greens. Use it in Umeboshi Broccoli (page 98) and Watercress Salad (page 101). You can find umeboshi paste at your local Asian market or health food store.

Makes 1 cup

¼ **cup umeboshi paste**

2 **scallions, coarsely chopped**

1 **cup watercress, washed**

Juice of 1 lemon (approximately ¼ cup)

½ **cup sesame oil (raw, not toasted)**

In food processor, combine all ingredients except the oil. Purée ingredients well. With food processor still running, slowly drizzle in sesame oil. Either use immediately or store, refrigerated, in a glass jar for up to 1 week.

CAESAR SALAD DRESSING

In a rush •• Vegetarian

This is our version of the classic Caesar. For the most part, it's the same as your traditional Caesar, with only one change: It doesn't feature anchovies, so it's usable by vegetarians. Instead, we recommend that you add anchovies directly to the salad; see our recipe for Caesar Salad (page 144).

Don't be put off by the fact that this dressing uses only the yolk of the egg. The yolk is the most nutritionally dense part of the egg, containing all the vitamins and antioxidants, plus good fats and cholesterol (both of which are important in the absorption and assimilation of the vitamins in the egg, which are fat-soluble).

Because this recipe uses raw egg and nothing to preserve it, this dressing keeps for less time than most. Use it within 3 days.

Makes 1½ cups

> 1 egg yolk
>
> 2 cloves garlic, minced (you can use a zester for this)
>
> 1 teaspoon store-bought or homemade Mustard (page 67) (Dijon or grainy; either is fine)
>
> ¼ cup lemon juice
>
> 2 tablespoons red wine vinegar
>
> ½ teaspoon sea salt
>
> ¼ teaspoon freshly ground pepper
>
> ¾ cup extra-virgin olive oil
>
> ½ cup grated Parmesan cheese

Combine all ingredients except oil and Parmesan in a blender. Purée. With the blender still running, slowly drizzle in olive oil and continue to blend until well mixed. Add cheese and continue processing until fully blended.

Use immediately or store in a glass jar in the refrigerator for up to 3 days.

VEGAN CAESAR DRESSING

Everyday •• Vegan •• Make it once, use it lots

For our vegan friends and those simply not comfortable with raw eggs, this is a great alternative to the classic Caesar. It's lighter but still packed with flavor. Because it doesn't use raw eggs, it also keeps for longer.

Makes 1½ cups

> 2 cloves garlic, peeled
>
> Juice from 2 lemons (approximately ½ cup)
>
> 1 teaspoon store-bought or homemade Mustard (page 67)
>
> 1 tablespoon gluten-free tamari soy sauce
>
> 1 tablespoon mellow white miso paste
>
> 1 teaspoon balsamic vinegar
>
> ¼ teaspoon sea salt
>
> 1 tablespoon nutritional yeast
>
> ¼ teaspoon freshly ground pepper
>
> ¾ cup extra-virgin olive oil

Combine all ingredients except olive oil in a blender, and turn the blender on to low. With the blender still running, slowly drizzle in the olive oil. As you're adding the oil, you can slowly turn the blender up to approximately medium level. When all oil has been added, turn blender up to high to make sure everything has been puréed.

Either use immediately or store in a glass jar in the refrigerator until ready to use. Keeps for up to 1 week.

Note: Because this dressing uses olive oil, it will solidify when you put it in the fridge. Remember to let it sit at room temperature for 10 to 15 minutes before use.

HONEY-LESS MUSTARD DRESSING

Everyday •• Vegan •• Make it once, use it lots

Our take on the classic honey mustard dressing has no honey. It uses pitted dates for sweetness instead. This dressing goes well with any green salad and can also be used as a marinade for chicken.

Makes 1 cup

½ **cup peeled and coarsely chopped cucumber**

3 **tablespoons raw unfiltered apple cider vinegar**

2 **tablespoons store-bought or homemade Mustard (page 67)**

2 **tablespoons gluten-free tamari soy sauce**

3 **tablespoons flaxseed oil**

3 **to 4 pitted dates**

½ **cup extra-virgin olive oil**

Pinch freshly ground pepper

Combine cucumber, vinegar, mustard, tamari, flaxseed oil, and dates in a blender and blend until smooth. With blender still running, slowly drizzle in olive oil until thoroughly combined. Add a pinch of pepper to taste.

Store in a jar in the fridge until ready to use. Keeps for about 1 week.

Note: Because this dressing uses olive oil, it will solidify when you put it in the fridge. Remember to let it sit at room temperature for 10 to 15 minutes before use.

THAI PEANUT SAUCE

Everyday •• Vegan •• Make it once, use it lots

This peanut sauce actually tastes like peanuts, unlike some commercial varieties. We use it with Chicken Satay (page 182), with Teriyaki Tempeh (page 178), and cold on our Asian Fusion Salad (page 116). You can also use it as a dip for veggies.

Makes 2½ cups

> 1 cup organic peanut butter (unsalted and with no additional oils or seasonings—just ground-up peanuts)
>
> 2 cloves garlic
>
> ½ cup store-bought or homemade Coconut Milk (page 44)
>
> 1 tablespoon coconut sugar or maple syrup
>
> Juice of 1 lime (approximately 2 tablespoons)
>
> 1 Persian cucumber, peeled
>
> 1 tablespoon minced cilantro
>
> 1 tablespoon chili flakes
>
> 2 tablespoons gluten-free tamari soy sauce

Put all ingredients in blender. Pulse until smooth. Add up to ½ cup filtered water as needed to achieve desired consistency. Store in a glass jar in the fridge. Keeps for up to 1 week.

TOMATILLO AVOCADO SAUCE

Everyday •• Vegan •• Make it once, use it lots

This can be used as a dressing, dip, or sauce on just about any Mexican-inspired dish. We often pair it with Mexican Salad (page 124). It's lighter than a guacamole, but creamier than your usual salsa. It's definitely a favorite around our house. We even use it on poached eggs with black beans and steamed greens for breakfast.

Makes 2 cups

   1 pound tomatillos

   ½ onion, sliced lengthwise

   1 jalapeño pepper, seeded

   2 tablespoons extra-virgin olive oil

   ½ packed cup fresh cilantro, stems removed

   1 tablespoon fresh lime juice

   ½ avocado, flesh scooped out

   ¾ teaspoon sea salt

Preheat oven to 395°F.

Remove stems and husks from the tomatillos and rinse them to remove their sticky film. Place the tomatillos, onion slices, and jalapeño pepper on an oven tray and bake for 15 minutes, until soft.

Remove the vegetables from the heat and put them in a blender. Add the remaining ingredients and blend until smooth. Use immediately at room temperature or refrigerate and use cold.

CARROT GINGER DRESSING

Everyday •• Vegan •• Make it once, use it lots

This dressing is a light and flavorful one that goes particularly well with any Asian-style salad such as Asian Fusion Salad (page 116), Shaved Beet Arugula Salad (page 106), or Watercress Salad (page 101).

Makes 2 cups

- 2 carrots, coarsely chopped (approximately 1 cup)
- 2 tablespoons apple cider vinegar
- 2 tablespoons gluten-free tamari soy sauce
- ¼ cup fresh mint
- 3 pitted dates
- 1 (1-inch) piece of ginger, grated (approximately 1 tablespoon)
- 1 teaspoon toasted sesame oil
- 3 tablespoons flaxseed oil
- ½ cup unrefined sesame oil

Combine carrots, apple cider vinegar, tamari, mint, dates, ginger, toasted sesame oil, flaxseed oil, and ¼ cup water in a blender. Blend until smooth. With the blender still going, slowly add the unrefined sesame oil, and continue blending until smooth.

Stores in the refrigerator for up to 1 week.

HONEY MISO DRESSING

Everyday •• Vegan •• Make it once, use it lots

This is a nice and light dressing that's not too sweet. It complements Asian dishes well. Flaxseed oil has a very specific taste and doesn't work with just anything, but it works quite nicely with miso. We like to pair it with Omega-Rich Arugula Salad (page 111).

Makes 1½ cups

- ¼ cup apple cider vinegar
- 2 teaspoons store-bought or homemade Dijon Mustard (page 67)
- 2 teaspoons miso paste (use whatever type you have on hand: mellow white or red works well)
- 2 tablespoons gluten-free tamari soy sauce
- 1½ teaspoons raw honey
- 2 tablespoons sesame seeds
- ¼ cup sesame oil
- 2 tablespoons flaxseed oil

In a blender, combine vinegar, mustard, miso, tamari, honey, and sesame seeds. Add ⅓ cup filtered water. Pulse to blend into a paste. With the blender still running, slowly add the sesame and flaxseed oils. Blend until fully combined, and store in a glass jar in the refrigerator for up to 1 week until ready to use.

PUMPKIN-SEED VEGAN PESTO

Everyday •• Vegan •• Make it once, use it lots

This is a more affordable and vegan alternative to the classic pesto. Using pumpkin seeds or pepitas instead of the usual (and spendy) pine nuts brings down the cost, and replacing the Parmesan cheese with miso paste makes it vegan. Toss with a little additional olive oil to use as a salad dressing. We use it in Nut-Crusted Pesto Chicken (page 187) and on Mediterranean Veggie Pizza (page 185).

Makes ½ cup

  ¼ **cup pumpkin seeds or pepitas, presoaked and dehydrated or slow-roasted**

  2 **cloves garlic, peeled**

  1 **packed cup fresh basil**

  1 **packed cup fresh spinach**

  ½ **teaspoon sea salt**

  ¼ **teaspoon lemon zest**

  Pinch freshly ground pepper

  ¼ **cup extra-virgin olive oil**

  2 **teaspoons mellow white miso paste**

Combine pumpkin seeds, garlic, basil, spinach, sea salt, lemon zest, and pepper to taste in a food processor. Pulse to mince thoroughly. With the food processor still running, slowly pour in the olive oil. Let combine thoroughly. Add the miso paste last, mixing well.

Use immediately or store in a glass jar in the fridge. Stores for up to 1 week.

TERIYAKI SAUCE

Everyday •• *Vegan* •• *Make it once, use it lots*

Teriyaki sauces are often oversweetened and have many unnecessary additives. It's incredibly difficult to find commercially prepared versions that are even close to naked. Our version uses unsweetened apple juice, pineapple chunks, and apricots for sweetening, all much more naked than the sugars you'd typically find in a store-bought version. We use it with Teriyaki Beef and Broccoli Rabe (page 177), Teriyaki Tempeh (page 178), and Long Life Greens (page 108).

Makes 1 cup

> 1 teaspoon unrefined coconut oil
>
> ½ small onion, evenly sliced
>
> ½ cup unsweetened and unfiltered apple juice
>
> 4 apricots
>
> 2 tablespoons pineapple chunks, fresh or frozen
>
> ¼ cup gluten-free tamari soy sauce

Heat coconut oil in a medium skillet over medium heat. Sauté onion for 3 to 5 minutes, until translucent with a little color. Remove from heat and add to blender along with apple juice, apricots, pineapple, and tamari. Blend until well mixed.

Pour sauce into a half-pint glass jar and let stand to cool. Refrigerate until ready to use. Lasts for up to 1 week.

VEGAN HOLLANDAISE SAUCE

Impress the neighbors •• Vegan •• Make it once, use it lots

Traditional hollandaise sauce is made with egg yolks, butter, and lemon. It's rich and it's tricky to make because the yolks curdle easily. Our version is lighter without losing any of the flavor—and is much easier to make. Use it with Portobello Eggs Benedict (page 90) for a delicious and nutritious twist on the classic bennie. It also makes a delicious sauce for Roasted Asparagus (page 114).

Makes 1 cup

>   1 tablespoon extra-virgin olive oil
>
>   1 small onion, thinly sliced lengthwise
>
>   ½ teaspoon sea salt
>
>   Juice of 1 lemon (approximately ¼ cup)
>
>   ½ teaspoon ground turmeric

Heat olive oil in medium skillet over medium-low heat. Add onion and salt, and cook slowly for 20 to 30 minutes, until onions brown. Don't overstir. The onions are caramelizing, and this is best achieved without disturbing them.

Put caramelized onions in a blender. Add lemon juice, turmeric, and 2 tablespoons filtered water. Blend until smooth. If needed, add a little more water, 1 teaspoon at a time, to have sauce reach desired consistency. Use immediately while still warm.

SPROUTED CILANTRO JALAPEÑO HUMMUS

Impress the neighbors •• Vegan •• Better than naked •• Make it once, use it lots

Hummus is usually made with garbanzo beans, tahini, lemon juice, garlic, and olive oil. This hummus is a significant deviation from that classic recipe and spices things up a bit on all fronts. For one, we've swapped out the cooked garbanzo beans for raw, sprouted adzuki beans. We chose adzuki beans, but you can use just about any large bean that's been sprouted. Try the traditional garbanzo or even white beans. Sprouting increases the nutritional value of the hummus significantly.

We've used lime, jalapeño, and cilantro to add a slight Mexican twist and some spice. This recipe is delicious with raw veggie sticks like carrots, celery, cucumber, peppers, and sugar snap peas, or you can have it on Zesty Crackers (page 222) or Sea Crackers (page 224).

Makes 1 cup

1 cup sprouted adzuki beans (for sprouting instructions, see page 32)

Juice of 1 lime (approximately 2 tablespoons)

1 jalapeño, seeded and coarsely chopped (leave some of the seeds in for a spicier hummus)

½ teaspoon sea salt

1 tablespoon tahini (for a fully raw recipe, use tahini made from raw sesame seeds)

½ cup extra-virgin olive oil

½ cup cilantro

Combine all ingredients except olive oil and cilantro in a food processor and process until it attains a creamy consistency. With the processor still running, slowly drizzle in the olive oil. Add the cilantro last, and process just until the cilantro has been blended into the hummus. Use immediately or store in a covered glass jar in the fridge until ready to use. Will keep for a little over a week.

10
Soups and Stews

You don't have to wait until winter to make soups and stews. They're a "make it once, use it lots" type of recipe. Perfect for a busy schedule. Soups and stews are gloriously versatile, good as a meal or a snack. Make a big batch on the weekend and use it throughout the week. Soups also freeze well, so try a few recipes and don't worry about there being too much left over.

We've got a whole variety of soups, from chilled and raw to more complex and that take longer to cook. We recommend that you use a homemade stock as your base—we have recipes for several versions in the "Basics" chapter. If you're not able to make your own stock, make sure you get an organic stock that's low in sodium.

RAW CUCUMBER MINT SOUP

In a rush •• Vegan •• Raw

This is an incredibly easy and fast raw soup. It's an ideal summer soup, with the cooling properties of the mint and cucumber. Delicious! It goes really well with Ceviche Choroni (page 202) or Quinoa Vegetable Sushi (page 200).

Makes 2 servings

  2 cucumbers, peeled and coarsely chopped (approximately 2 cups)

  1 avocado, flesh scooped out and pit discarded

  Juice of 2 large limes (approximately ¼ cup)

  2 packed tablespoons fresh mint

  1 teaspoon sliced green onion, greens only

  ½ teaspoon sea salt

  Pinch chili powder

Combine cucumber, avocado, lime juice, mint, green onion, and sea salt in a blender, and purée until smooth. Serve topped with a pinch of chili powder to taste. Eat at room temperature, or refrigerate and eat cold.

NO-FRILLS MISO SOUP

In a rush •• Pescatarian, with vegetarian and vegan options

Miso soup is very fast and nourishing. It has immune-boosting properties and is actually considered a medicinal soup in some Asian cultures. Its simplicity and speed make it an excellent choice when you're under the weather and needing something quick and warming. For maximum nutritional value, we recommend making it with stock, but it's possible to use water as well.

This recipe uses seaweed, which you can find at your local Asian market or health food store.

For a vegetarian version of this soup, use Kitchen Scraps Veggie Stock and for a vegan version of this soup, use water instead of broth or stock.

Makes 2 servings

> 2 tablespoons wakame seaweed
>
> 2½ cups Fish Stock (page 48), Dashi (page 59), Kitchen Scraps Veggie Stock (page 50), or water
>
> 2 tablespoons red miso paste (red miso is ideal, but use whatever kind of miso paste you have on hand)
>
> 1 tablespoon sliced scallions, greens only

In medium saucepan, heat wakame seaweed and fish stock or veggie broth over high heat. When boiling, turn off heat and whisk in miso. Serve immediately with scallions sprinkled on top.

Note: Make sure not to boil the soup once you've added the miso. The healthy and cultured properties of the miso will be destroyed if it's heated to boiling.

WHITE BEAN LEEK SOUP

In a rush •• Vegetarian •• Make it once, use it lots

This is a lower-starch variation of traditional potato leek soup, but with the same creamy texture. We've replaced the potatoes with white beans, which are higher in fiber and protein. It's delicious hot but can also be eaten cold. If you're eating it cold simply let the soup cool, then refrigerate, covered, for 1 to 2 hours.

Makes 4 servings

- 1 tablespoon ghee
- 1 cup thinly chopped leeks, white parts only
- 2 cloves garlic, minced
- 1 teaspoon sea salt
- 3 cups presoaked and cooked white beans or 2 (15-ounce) cans white beans, drained and rinsed well (great northern, cannellini, and navy beans are all good options)
- 1 cup Kitchen Scraps Veggie Stock (page 50)
- 1 cup whole cream
- 1 teaspoon tarragon
- 1 teaspoon rosemary
- 1 tablespoon lemon juice

In a medium saucepan, heat the ghee over medium heat. Add the leeks and garlic with the sea salt and sauté for 2 to 3 minutes, just until they've got a little color.

While the leeks and garlic are sautéing, combine the beans and the stock in a blender and purée. When the leeks have some color, add the blended beans and stock to the pot. Add the cream, tarragon, and rosemary, and stir well. Cook for another 2 to 3 minutes to heat the soup. Once the soup has been heated, remove from heat, add lemon juice, and stir well. Serve immediately.

TOMATO BASIL SOUP

In a rush •• Vegetarian •• Make it once, use it lots

Who doesn't love the homey comfort of a bowl of hot tomato soup? This light and flavorful recipe is a welcome change from the bread-laden, heavy-creamed traditional tomato soups. It goes well with Caesar Salad (page 123), Pesto Vegetable Linguini (page 190), or Nut-Crusted Pesto Chicken (page 187).

Makes 4 servings

> 1 cup Kitchen Scraps Veggie Stock (page 50)
>
> 6 to 7 Roma tomatoes, peeled and seeded or 1 (28-ounce) can whole tomatoes
>
> 1 clove garlic, peeled and coarsely chopped
>
> 2 packed tablespoons fresh basil
>
> 1 teaspoon balsamic vinegar
>
> 1 scallion, white and green part separated
>
> Sea salt (if using canned tomatoes, you can omit this if they contain sodium)

In a medium saucepan, heat stock over medium heat. While stock is heating, combine tomatoes, garlic, basil, balsamic vinegar, and the white part from the scallion in a blender. Purée until smooth.

Add the tomato purée and salt to taste to the veggie stock and stir. Cook for 5 minutes, until warmed. Serve with greens from the scallion chopped finely and sprinkled over top as a garnish.

CREAMY TARRAGON PEA SOUP

In a rush •• Vegetarian •• Make it once, use it lots

This is another speedy blender soup, one made even faster by use of any leftover Cuban Green Peas. This soup goes really well with Noodle-less Lasagna (page 192) or Wild Rice Salad (page 117).

Makes 3 to 4 servings

> 1 cup Kitchen Scraps Veggie Stock (page 50)
>
> 1 cup Cuban Green Peas (page 100)
>
> 1 tablespoon tarragon
>
> 1 clove garlic, peeled and coarsely chopped
>
> ¼ teaspoon sea salt
>
> 2 tablespoons cream
>
> Dash paprika

In a medium saucepan, heat stock over medium heat. While stock is heating, combine Cuban Green Peas, tarragon, garlic, and sea salt in blender and purée until smooth.

Add green pea mixture to saucepan and stir to mix. Cook for 5 minutes to warm through. Add cream just before serving and stir to mix well. Garnish with a dash of paprika.

CURRIED LENTIL SOUP

Everyday •• Vegan, with vegetarian option •• Make it once, use it lots

This is an easy and delicious no-frills curried lentil soup. Much of the time involved is unattended. It goes well with brown rice and sautéed veggies. For the vegetarian version of this soup, use Kitchen Scraps Veggie Stock instead of water as a base.

Makes 4 servings

> **2 teaspoons unrefined coconut oil**
>
> **½ cup finely diced onion**
>
> **½ teaspoon sea salt**
>
> **¼ teaspoon ground turmeric**
>
> **½ teaspoon curry powder**
>
> **1 teaspoon fennel seeds**
>
> **¼ teaspoon ground coriander**
>
> **½ teaspoon cumin seeds**
>
> **1 cup red lentils (or whatever lentils you have)**
>
> **2½ cups water or Kitchen Scraps Veggie Stock (page 50)**
>
> **1 tablespoon lemon juice**
>
> **½ cup store-bought or homemade Coconut Milk (page 44)**

Heat coconut oil in a large saucepan over medium heat. Add the onions, sea salt, turmeric, curry powder, fennel seeds, coriander, and cumin seeds, and sauté for 1 to 2 minutes, until onion is translucent. Add lentils and the water or stock. Cover and bring to a boil. With lid still on, turn heat down to low and let simmer for 20 to 25 minutes, until lentils have been cooked through. Remove from heat.

Pour lentils into a blender, add lemon juice and coconut milk, and blend well. Serve warm.

HEARTY MISO SOUP

Everyday •• Vegan

This soup is another favorite at our house. It's an excellent winter soup, as it's a great immunity booster and is very alkalinizing and soothing—all important qualities during cold and flu season. Unlike our No-Frills Miso Soup (page 157), this soup is quite hearty and rich with vegetables. The addition of the Quinoa makes it a full meal.

This recipe uses seaweed, which you can find at your local Asian market or health food store.

Makes 2 servings

> 2 teaspoons unrefined coconut oil
>
> ½ cup thinly sliced yellow onion
>
> 2 cloves garlic, thinly sliced
>
> ½ cup sliced carrot
>
> 3 fresh shiitake mushrooms, sliced
>
> ⅔ cup cooked Quinoa (page 54)
>
> 2 tablespoons arame, hijiki, or wakame seaweed
>
> 1 to 2 tablespoons miso paste (red miso is most flavorful for this recipe, but use whatever you have)
>
> 1 cup thinly sliced bok choy or napa cabbage
>
> 1 teaspoon gluten-free tamari soy sauce
>
> 2 tablespoons sliced scallions
>
> Dulse flakes, for garnish (optional)

In a medium saucepan, heat the oil over medium heat. Add the onion and sauté for 5 minutes, until it begins to brown. Add the garlic and continue to sauté for 30 seconds, stirring a couple of times. Add the carrot and mushrooms, and sauté for another 2 minutes. Add 2½ cups filtered water, cover, and simmer over medium-low heat for 5 minutes. Remove from heat.

Add the Quinoa and arame to the soup and stir to combine. Measure the miso into a small bowl and add ½ cup of the hot soup from the pot to the bowl. Using a whisk, dissolve the miso into the liquid and return the mixture to the saucepan. Do not boil or simmer the miso, as this destroys the beneficial microorganisms.

Add the bok choy and the tamari to the pot, and stir to combine until bok choy is lightly wilted. Pour soup into two bowls and garnish with the scallions and dulse flakes.

BORSCHT

Everyday •• Vegetarian, with vegan option •• Make it once, use it lots

Borscht—beet soup—is an Eastern European soup that's delicious both hot and cold. It's the ideal all-season soup. Add a dollop of crème fraîche or plain yogurt to take it over the top. For a vegan version of this soup, substitute coconut oil for ghee, substitute water for Kitchen Scraps Veggie Stock, and omit the crème fraîche.

Makes 6 servings

> 1 tablespoon ghee or unrefined coconut oil
>
> 1 onion, diced (approximately 1 cup)
>
> 1 sweet potato, peeled and grated (approximately 1 cup)
>
> 1 teaspoon sea salt
>
> 2 red beets, washed and grated (approximately 2 cups)
>
> 2 cups shredded red cabbage
>
> 6 cups Kitchen Scraps Veggie Stock (page 50) or water
>
> 2 tablespoons raw apple cider vinegar
>
> 1 tablespoon dried dill
>
> **Crème fraîche, sour cream, or plain yogurt (optional)**

Heat ghee in bottom of 5-quart soup pot. Add onion and cook for 2 to 3 minutes, until translucent. Add sweet potato, sprinkle with ¼ teaspoon sea salt, and continue cooking for another 3 to 5 minutes. Add beets and continue cooking for another 2 to 3 minutes. Add cabbage and continue cooking for 2 to 3 minutes more.

Pour in stock, add another ¼ teaspoon of salt, cover, and bring to a boil. Turn heat down to low, and let simmer, covered, for about 15 minutes. Remove from heat and add the apple cider vinegar. Using a hand blender, blend the soup to desired thickness. We like to leave some chunks in it. Stir in dill and remaining ½ teaspoon salt (you might go slowly with the salt so that you can stop if it gets too salty for your taste; how much salt you need will depend on whether you used water, homemade stock, or store-bought stock).

Serve hot with a big dollop of crème fraîche. Or chill and serve cold, also with a dollop of crème fraîche.

Tip: Grating beets can lead to grating your fingers, which is never fun. Here's a tip to make life easier: Keep about an inch of the stem attached and use it as a handle to hold the beet as you're grating it. This will keep your fingers safely away from the grater—and keep your fingers from getting too stained.

VEGETABLE TEMPEH CHILI

Impress the neighbors •• Vegetarian, with vegan options

This is a hearty vegetarian version of a meat chili. The tempeh—fermented soybeans formed into blocks—substitutes for the beef quite well and makes for a warming and filling meal. For a vegan version of this recipe, substitute coconut oil for the ghee and omit the cheese.

Makes 3 servings

1 (8 oz) package tempeh

2 tablespoons ghee or unrefined coconut oil

1 onion, diced (about 1 cup)

Sea salt

2 cloves garlic, minced (about 2 tablespoons)

2 carrots, grated (about 1 cup)

2 tablespoons chili powder

2 tablespoons ground cumin

1 red pepper, stemmed, seeded, and diced

1 yellow pepper, stemmed, seeded, and diced

1 green pepper, stemmed, seeded, and diced

2 dried chiles (our favorite is dried chipotle)

2 (28-ounce) cans diced tomatoes, with juice

2 teaspoons dried oregano

1 teaspoon fennel seeds (optional)

2 yellow squash, quartered lengthwise and diced (1 cup)

2 zucchini, quartered lengthwise and diced (1 cup)

Freshly ground black pepper

1½ cups kidney beans, presoaked and cooked or 1 (15-ounce) can kidney beans, drained and rinsed

1½ cups black beans, presoaked and cooked or 1 (15-ounce) can black beans, drained and rinsed

1 cup thinly sliced kale

¼ cup finely chopped flat-leaf parsley

½ cup grated sharp cheddar cheese (optional)

Using your hands, crumble the tempeh into small bits in a medium bowl and set aside. Melt the ghee in a heavy pot over medium heat. Add the onions and a pinch of salt, and sauté for 1 minute, then add tempeh and cook, stirring, for 10 minutes, until some browning occurs, adding the garlic and carrots in the last 2 minutes. Reduce the heat to low; stir in chili powder and cumin. Cook for 1 minute longer. Stir in the bell peppers, dried chiles, tomatoes, oregano, and fennel seeds. Bring to a boil, reduce the heat to medium, and let simmer, partially covered, for 15 minutes, stirring occasionally.

Add the squash and zucchini. Season with salt and pepper, and adjust the other seasonings as needed. Stir in the kidney beans and black beans. Simmer, uncovered, for 15 minutes longer, until the vegetables are tender, stirring occasionally. Add kale in the last 5 minutes and mix well.

Serve hot, garnished with cheddar cheese and parsley.

CARROT GINGER SOUP

Everyday •• Vegetarian, with vegan option

Carrot ginger soup is such a warming and nourishing soup for the cold winter months. We've mixed it up a little in this version by adding some parsnips. This is an excellent starter for a roast dinner such as Roast Beef (page 195) or Asian Roasted Chicken (page 188). For a vegan version of this soup, substitute water for Kitchen Scraps Veggie Stock.

Makes 4 small servings

> 1 tablespoon unrefined coconut oil
>
> 3 cups evenly sliced (into rounds) carrot
>
> 1 cup evenly sliced (into rounds) parsnips
>
> 1 small onion, coarsely chopped
>
> 3 to 4 cups Kitchen Scraps Veggie Stock (page 50) or water
>
> 2 tablespoons grated ginger
>
> 2 teaspoons gluten-free tamari soy sauce
>
> 1 tablespoon thinly sliced Thai basil (optional)

Preheat oven to 400°F. If your kitchen is cool and the coconut oil is solid, put it in the oven in a heat-resistant bowl to melt as the oven is heating. Toss the carrots, parsnips, and onion with the coconut oil, and roast for 20 minutes.

Put cooked carrots, parsnips, and onions in blender along with 3 cups of the stock and purée until smooth. With blender still going, add ginger and tamari, and blend until well mixed. Slowly add more stock if a thinner consistency is desired. Garnish each serving with Thai basil, and serve warm.

MOROCCAN CHICKEN STEW

Impress the neighbors •• Omnivore

Moroccan flavors are a nice change from the usual. The flavors—similar to a curry with the addition of cinnamon and lemon—are very warming and nourishing. This recipe uses dark meat, the fattier and more flavorful part of the chicken. Serve with Stephanie's Family Rice (page 55) or your grain of choice.

Makes 4 servings

- 2 teaspoons ghee
- 1 onion, diced
- 2 cloves garlic, minced (approximately 1 tablespoon)
- 1 teaspoon paprika
- 1 teaspoon cinnamon
- 1 teaspoon ground cumin
- ½ teaspoon ground coriander
- ½ teaspoon ground turmeric
- 2 teaspoons grated ginger
- 10 ounces dark-meat chicken, chopped into bite-size pieces
- 1 large zucchini, grated (approximately 2 cups)
- 1 small carrot, grated (approximately ½ cup)
- 1 (28-ounce) can diced tomatoes
- 1½ cups garbanzo beans, presoaked and precooked, or 1 (15-ounce) can garbanzo beans, well rinsed
- 1 lemon, one half of it juiced (approximately 2 tablespoons) and the other half cut into rounds and seeded (approximately 4 slices)

Heat the ghee in a large soup pot over low heat. Sauté the onions and garlic for 2 to 3 minutes, until onion is translucent. Add paprika, cinnamon, cumin, coriander, turmeric, and ginger, and stir to mix well. Add the chicken, zucchini, and carrot, and continue to sauté for another 2 minutes. Add tomatoes, garbanzo beans, lemon juice, and sliced lemons. Cover, turn heat up to high, and bring to a boil. Turn heat down to low, keeping the pot covered, and let simmer for 15 to 20 minutes, until chicken is cooked. Serve warm.

CURRIED LAMB STEW

Impress the neighbors •• Omnivore

This is a deeply warming and nourishing stew, ideally eaten in front of a soothing fire on a cold winter night. The curry sauce is made separately from the stew, so if you like it, here's a time-saving tip: Next time you make this stew, double up on the sauce ingredients and save half of it, frozen, for another curry later on.

Makes 6 servings

- 1 tablespoon plus 1 teaspoon ghee

- 1 teaspoon sea salt

- 1 large head cauliflower, roughly chopped (approximately 4 to 6 cups)

- 1 onion, diced

- ½ teaspoon ground turmeric

- 1 teaspoon curry powder

- ½ teaspoon ground cumin

- ¼ teaspoon freshly ground pepper

- 2 pitted dates

- ½ cup store-bought or homemade Coconut Milk (page 44)

- Juice of ½ lime (approximately ½ tablespoon)

- 1 clove garlic, minced

- 1 large shallot, thinly sliced (approximately ¼ cup)

- 5 to 6 crimini mushrooms, thinly sliced (approximately ½ cup)

- 8 ounces boneless stewing lamb

- 1 small zucchini, grated (approximately ½ cup)

- 1 heaping cup chopped (into 1-inch pieces) sugar snap peas (optional; substitute frozen green peas if fresh snap peas aren't available)

- 3 cups cooked brown rice (optional)

To make the curry sauce, preheat oven to 385°F. Put 1 tablespoon of ghee in a large heat-resistant mixing bowl and into the preheating oven for 1 to 2 minutes, until melted. Remove the bowl from the oven and add ½ teaspoon of the sea salt, cauliflower, and diced onion, and mix well to coat the cauliflower with the ghee. Spread out on an oven tray and roast for 15 to 20 minutes, until soft.

When cauliflower has been cooked through, remove tray from the oven. Place about half the onion and cauliflower mixture into a blender with the turmeric, the remaining ½ teaspoon of sea salt, curry powder, cumin, pepper, dates, coconut milk, and lime juice. Blend until smooth. Set aside.

Heat the remaining 1 teaspoon ghee in large skillet over medium heat. Sauté garlic, shallots, and mushrooms for 2 to 3 minutes, until just soft. Add the lamb and brown it 5 to 6 minutes. Add the zucchini and sauté for another 1 minute. Add the remainder of the roasted cauliflower and onion, and stir to mix. Add the curry sauce, adding a little water if needed (up to ½ cup), cover, and let simmer for 15 minutes, stirring periodically. Just before serving, add sugar snap peas, and let sit in curry for 2 minutes to warm.

Serve as is or over brown rice.

11
Entrées

The "Entrées" chapter is where we've put many of the meat and fish dishes. They're designed to perfectly complement the salads, sides, soups, and sauces from the other chapters.

A lot of these recipes fall in the "impress the neighbors" category because they take longer to make, but in many cases this additional time is unattended. Only in a few instances do you really need to be involved in the recipe for more than half an hour.

When you're preparing a dish that's protein based, as many of these entrées are, we recommend making more than you need and using leftovers in lunches. For example, Asian Roasted Chicken (page 188) or Roast Beef (page 195) will give you enough meat to last several days—and can of course be used in creative ways in salads, in wraps, or even as snacks. This is an excellent, naked solution to sandwich meat, because it's fresh and without the nitrates, sugar, sodium, and extra preservatives so often found in packaged deli meat.

SEARED TUNA

In a rush •• Pescatarian

Searing tuna is a fast and easy way to prepare the fish fresh. It kills any pathogens that may live on the surface of the fish, while leaving most of the fish raw. This cooking style protects the delicate essential fatty acids that go rancid with heat. This means you get the health benefits of raw fish without the risks. This recipe goes well with Kale Arame Salad (page 96), Umeboshi Broccoli (page 98), or Watercress Salad (page 101).

Makes 3 servings

2 teaspoons unrefined coconut oil

10 ounces sushi-grade ahi tuna

⅛ teaspoon sea salt

Heat a large skillet over medium-high heat. Add the coconut oil and let melt. While oil is melting, sprinkle both sides of the tuna with sea salt.

Sear the tuna on the top and bottom for 2 minutes each. An easy way to know when each side has been seared sufficiently is to watch the color of the tuna on the edges. As you sear the bottom, the flesh on the edges will start to turn white, starting from the bottom and moving up the side of the fish. Before the white has reached the middle of the fish, it's time to flip it. While the other side is searing, watch for the white to start at the bottom and move up the edge of the fish. Before it meets the white in the middle from searing the other side, it's ready. Remove from heat and allow to rest for 2 to 3 minutes before slicing.

Tip: To prevent cross-contamination and shorten cleanup time, keep fish (or any meat) on the wrapping it came in while preparing it. This keeps you from having to clean and wash a cutting board.

SAUTÉED CHICKEN WITH LEMON AND HERBS

In a rush •• Omnivore

This is a good example of a speedy main course. It's delicious and so flavorful, and takes very little time to prepare. We like to serve it with a nice big green salad like Speedy Green Salad (page 103).

Makes 2 servings

- 1 tablespoon ghee
- 2 small chicken breasts, approximately 4 to 5 ounces each
- 1 teaspoon granulated garlic
- ½ teaspoon sea salt
- ½ teaspoon freshly ground pepper
- Zest and juice of 1 lemon
- 1 teaspoon minced parsley
- Dash paprika

Heat ghee in large skillet over medium heat. While the ghee is heating, butterfly the chicken breasts. Lay the breasts out on a large plate. Sprinkle ½ teaspoon of the garlic, ¼ teaspoon of the sea salt, and ¼ teaspoon of the pepper over the top of the chicken breasts.

When skillet is hot, put chicken in the skillet, seasoned side down. Cook for 5 minutes. Just before flipping the chicken, season the side of the chicken that's facing up with the remaining garlic, remaining sea salt, and remaining pepper. Flip the chicken; add 1 tablespoon filtered water; sprinkle with lemon zest, parsley, and a dash of paprika; cover skillet; and cook for another 3 to 4 minutes, until nicely browned and cooked through. Serve warm with lemon juice drizzled on top.

LENTIL CURRY

In a rush •• Vegan

Lentils are a good source of vegetarian protein, more digestible than most beans. They marry well with curry flavors. This simple dish can stand on its own or is delicious paired with some Coconut Rice (page 52).

Makes 4 servings

- 1 tablespoon unrefined coconut oil
- ½ onion, diced
- ¼ teaspoon sea salt
- ½ teaspoon cumin seeds
- 1 tablespoon curry powder
- 1 zucchini, grated
- 2 cups thinly sliced Swiss chard (use the stalk as well)
- 2 cups store-bought or homemade Lentils (page 46), rinsed, drained, and precooked

In a large skillet, heat coconut oil over medium heat. Sauté onion, salt, cumin, and curry powder for 2 to 3 minutes, until onions are translucent. Add zucchini and sauté for another 2 minutes. Add chard and sauté for another 2 to 3 minutes, until just wilted.

Combine veggies with cooked lentils and serve warm.

SESAME-CRUSTED SALMON

In a rush •• Pescatarian

This is a really fast salmon dish that's sure to impress. It pairs nicely with any quick salad—like Speedy Green Salad (page 103) or Raw Kale and Cabbage Salad (page 105)—steamed greens, or any sautéed veggies. It's delicious, easy, and remarkably quick to make.

Makes 2 servings

> 1 teaspoon unrefined coconut oil
>
> 1 (10-ounce) piece wild salmon
>
> 1 teaspoon sesame oil
>
> 1 tablespoon raw sesame seeds
>
> ½ teaspoon gluten-free tamari soy sauce
>
> ½ teaspoon toasted sesame oil (optional)
>
> Juice of 1 lime (about 2 tablespoons)
>
> 1 sprig cilantro, dill, or parsley (optional)

Preheat broiler on high.

Using an oven-safe skillet, heat the coconut oil over medium heat. While skillet is heating, rub salmon with sesame oil and sprinkle each side with sesame seeds.

When pan is hot, cook salmon skin side up for 2 minutes. Then put salmon under broiler for another 2 to 3 minutes, until done. We recommend not overcooking the salmon, as that can damage some of the good fatty acids in the fish. Remove from oven and then from pan using a metal spatula.

Drizzle tamari, toasted sesame oil, and lime juice over the top of the fish, and serve warm with a sprig of cilantro, dill, or parsley.

BROILED SARDINES

In a rush •• Pescatarian

Sardines are one of those great fishes with a bad rap. The typical response to a recommendation for eating them is a scrunched-up nose and look of disgust. On the fish spectrum, sardines are a very sustainable and healthy option because they're low on the food chain (which means minimal methylmercury and PCB contamination) and they're plentiful (so we're not depleting already-depleted fish stocks). They also happen to be very high in those all-important omega-3 essential fatty acids and super-easy to cook.

This recipe is an easy and delicious way to prepare them. If you've decided you're not a sardine person, we encourage you to try this anyway. You might surprise yourself.

This dish pairs nicely with Umeboshi Broccoli (page 98). Use a little of the Umeboshi Dressing (page 143) from the broccoli on the sardines as well.

Makes 2 servings

> **4 fresh sardines, wild caught**
>
> **1 tablespoon melted ghee or butter**
>
> **Juice of 1 lemon (approximately 4 tablespoons)**
>
> **Sea salt**
>
> **Freshly ground pepper**

Set broiler to high. While broiler is heating, wash the fish. Leaving them whole (or, if that's too much for you, you can cut the heads off) put them on an oven tray and drizzle melted ghee and half of the lemon juice over them.

Broil the fish for 2 to 3 minutes on each side. Remove from oven, season with sea salt and pepper to taste, and serve immediately. Drizzle with the other half of the lemon juice to taste.

Tip: When you eat the sardines, pull the meat gently off the bones with a fork. The easiest way to do this is to grab the fish by the tail, insert your fork just under the gills, and scrape down toward the tail. Sometimes sardine bones are small enough to eat, but be careful! We don't want anyone getting a fish bone stuck somewhere.

TERIYAKI BEEF AND BROCCOLI RABE

In a rush •• Omnivore

This is a very speedy and easy dinner that makes use of still-frozen beef. It's excellent for those days when you forgot to pull the meat out of the freezer for dinner until the last moment. You slice the frozen beef thinly, taking advantage of the fact that it's hard as a rock.

Makes 4 servings

> **12 to 16 ounces grass-fed beef steak, frozen (flat iron, rib eye, and sirloin are all good options)**
>
> **1 to 2 teaspoons unrefined coconut oil**
>
> **1 shallot, thinly sliced**
>
> **2 cups coarsely chopped broccoli rabe**
>
> **½ cup Teriyaki Sauce (page 152)**
>
> **1 teaspoon red pepper flakes**
>
> **2 cups cooked Quinoa (page 54) (optional)**

Place the frozen beef on the counter for 10 to 15 minutes to defrost slightly. Using your chef's knife, shave the still-frozen meat into thin pieces. Heat the coconut oil in a large skillet over medium heat. Sauté the shallots for 1 minute, and then add the broccoli. Cook for 2 minutes, stirring occasionally. Add the beef and continue to sauté for another 2 to 3 minutes. Add the Teriyaki Sauce and cook for another 1 to 2 minutes, until sauce is just hot. Sprinkle with red pepper flakes and serve immediately either alone or with a side of Quinoa.

TERIYAKI TEMPEH

In a rush •• Vegan

Tempeh is one of the four forms of soy that's digestible by our bodies. Unlike tofu, it uses the whole bean and is fermented. This recipe is delicious paired with Long Life Greens (page 108).

Makes 2 to 3 servings

> **2 to 4 tablespoons unrefined coconut oil**
>
> **8 ounces tempeh, cut into ¼-inch-by-2-inch sticks**
>
> **½ teaspoon sea salt**
>
> **½ cup Teriyaki Sauce (page 152)**

Heat 2 tablespoons of coconut oil in a large skillet over medium heat. Add half the tempeh and ¼ teaspoon sea salt, and fry for 2 to 3 minutes, until golden brown on each side. Repeat with the other half of tempeh, adding remaining 2 tablespoons of oil if needed. When done, toss with Teriyaki Sauce and serve with greens.

SMELT FRY

Everyday •• Pescatarian

Similar to anchovies, smelt are an excellent tiny-fish option. Smelt are typically used as fish bait and can be eaten whole—head, guts, and all. Smelt are sustainable, affordable, and underfished, meaning you can eat them frequently and in good conscience. Fresh is preferable, but frozen is widely available. Buy them in bulk and eat them as snacks, in salads, or on pizza. We recommend trying them in Watercress Salad (page 101) with Umeboshi Dressing (page 143) or in Caesar Salad (page 123).

Makes 2 servings

- 2 tablespoons lemon juice
- 1 teaspoon thyme
- ½ teaspoon fennel seeds, lightly crushed
- ½ teaspoon red pepper flakes
- ½ teaspoon freshly ground black pepper
- 2 to 3 tablespoons ghee
- 3 ounces smelt, fresh or frozen
- ¼ to ½ cup arrowroot powder
- ½ to 1 teaspoon sea salt

Mix the lemon juice, thyme, crushed fennel, red pepper flakes, and black pepper in a small bowl and set aside.

Heat ghee in a medium skillet over medium-high heat. As ghee is heating, put arrowroot in a dish and dredge smelt (one at a time) on both sides. Shake off excess arrowroot and place smelt in hot ghee. You should hear a sizzling sound. As the smelt fries, repeat the dredging procedure on the next smelt and place in skillet, making sure not to crowd. Using tongs, flip each smelt until golden brown on each side. They should cook for approximately 1 minute per side.

Place the cooked smelt on a plate, season with salt, and serve warm. Drizzle lemon sauce over the crispy smelt right before serving, or place on table as a dipping sauce.

Note: Most smelt are so small that bones aren't a worry. For larger smelt beware of any small bones. We don't want anyone getting a fish bone stuck somewhere.

MAPLE SAGE-GLAZED PORK TENDERLOIN

Everyday •• Omnivore

This recipe is sure to wow your friends and family. It's an amazingly easy and surprisingly flavorful pork tenderloin. Since you've got the oven on already, it goes particularly well with roasted veggies of any kind. Our personal favorites are Roasted Asparagus (page 114) if it's springtime, and Roasted Brussels Sprouts (page 115) if it's wintertime.

Makes 4 servings

> **1 pound pork tenderloin**
>
> **Sea salt**
>
> **Freshly ground pepper**
>
> **1 tablespoon ghee**
>
> **¼ cup maple syrup, grade B or C**
>
> **1 teaspoon powdered sage**
>
> **2 tablespoons gluten-free tamari soy sauce**
>
> **1 tablespoon store-bought or homemade stone-ground Mustard (page 67)**

Preheat oven to 395°F.

Liberally sprinkle pork with sea salt and pepper to your liking. Heat ghee in large skillet over medium heat. Sear pork for 3 to 4 minutes each side so that each has some color. Place on an oven tray and bake for 10 minutes.

While pork is cooking, whisk together maple syrup, sage, tamari, and mustard in a small saucepan over medium-high heat. Reduce the sauce to a thick glaze, about 3 to 5 minutes. Set aside.

Remove pork from the oven and cut into 8 equal rounds (thickness will depend on the circumference of the tenderloin). Rounds should still have a pink hue to them. Using a spoon, cover the tenderloin rounds with half the sauce, coating well. Put tenderloins back on the oven tray and cook for another 5 to 7 minutes, until done.

Plate pork rounds and pour remaining sauce over top. Serve warm.

QUICK AND DIRTY BEEF STIR-FRY

Everyday •• Omnivore

This recipe is an excellent one for those days when you forget to pull the meat out of the freezer ahead of time. It uses still-frozen beef, which is shaved—sliced thinly—so it cooks really quickly.

Makes 4 servings

2 tablespoons unrefined coconut oil

1 clove garlic, thinly cut into rounds

1 heaping cup thinly sliced shiitake mushrooms

10-ounce grass-fed beef steak, frozen and left out to defrost for 10 to 15 minutes

5 leaves of large bok choy, thinly sliced, stems separated from leaves

1 carrot, grated

½ teaspoon finely grated ginger

3 tablespoons gluten-free tamari soy sauce

Juice of 1 lime (approximately 1 tablespoon)

½ cup store-bought or homemade Coconut Milk (page 44) (optional)

2 teaspoons coconut sugar (optional)

1 tablespoon sesame seeds (optional)

Heat coconut oil in a large skillet or wok. Add garlic and mushrooms, stirring to coat with oil. Cook for 3 to 4 minutes.

While garlic and mushrooms are cooking, slice the beef against the grain as thinly as possible. This is easier to do when it's still frozen. Add the beef to the skillet and cook for 3 to 4 minutes. Add the bok choy stems only (don't add the greens yet), grated carrot, and grated ginger, and cook for another 3 to 4 minutes. Every time you add more veggies, turn the heat up slightly to keep the pan hot.

Mix together the tamari, lime, coconut milk, and coconut sugar and add it to the pan along with the bok choy leaves. Stir, and cook for another 2 minutes, until bok choy leaves have just wilted. Serve alone or on a bed of whole-grain rice, sprinkled with sesame seeds.

Tip: Freeze fresh ginger ahead of time, and it'll be much easier to grate.

CHICKEN SATAY

Everyday •• Omnivore

This recipe makes use of a marinade to flavor and tenderize the chicken. Using a marinade takes a little forethought, but not much additional effort. You get quite a lot of return for a small time investment. We suggest that you let the meat marinate overnight, but you can let it sit for as little as 30 minutes and up to 24 hours.

We've included this recipe in the "everyday" category even though it does require marinating time, since most of that time is unattended.

Makes 4 servings

> 1 teaspoon ground cumin
>
> 1 teaspoon ground coriander
>
> 1 tablespoon ground turmeric
>
> 1 teaspoon ground ginger
>
> 1 teaspoon granulated garlic
>
> 1 teaspoon granulated onion
>
> 2 tablespoons coconut sugar
>
> 3 tablespoons gluten-free tamari soy sauce
>
> ⅓ cup store-bought or homemade Coconut Milk (page 44)
>
> ¼ cup sesame oil
>
> 1 pound boneless chicken, light or dark meat, chopped into bite-size pieces
>
> 1 recipe Thai Peanut Sauce (page 147)
>
> 8 to 12 skewer sticks (if wood or bamboo, presoak them in cold water)

Whisk together in a small bowl all ingredients except chicken and Thai Peanut Sauce.

Toss the chicken in the marinade, and leave it in a bowl, covered, in the refrigerator for 12 to 24 hours. Basically, the longer you marinate the chicken, the better.

Preheat oven to 395°F.

While oven is preheating, skewer chicken, 3 to 4 pieces to a skewer (or more, depending on the size of your skewers). Place on an oven tray and cook for 10 minutes. Remove the tray from oven, flip chicken using tongs, and put it back in the oven to cook for another 10 minutes. Serve with Thai Peanut Sauce. For crispier chicken, put it under the broiler for the last 2 to 3 minutes of cooking.

LIGHT AND CRISPY CHICKEN BITES

Everyday •• Omnivore

Indulge your desire for fried chicken with this remarkably easy recipe. It uses coconut oil, which handles the heat well without going rancid, and Brown Rice Fry Batter rather than your usual heavy and gluten-laden fare. Serve with something green, such as some lightly sautéed kale or asparagus.

Makes 4 servings

½ to 1 cup unrefined coconut oil (enough for about ½ inch in wok or sauté pan)

4 garlic cloves, cut into thin rounds

Salt

1 pound boneless, skinless chicken (breast or thigh meat is fine), cut into bite-size pieces

¾ cup cold Brown Rice Fry Batter (page 47)

Freshly ground pepper

1 teaspoon chili flakes (optional)

2 tablespoons minced cilantro, leaves only

1 tablespoon thinly sliced scallions, white and green parts

Heat coconut oil in a wok or sauté pan over medium heat. When the oil is hot (test by dropping one garlic round into the pan: the oil should bubble up around it), fry the garlic rounds until light brown and crispy. Remove garlic from pan with a slotted spoon and set aside. Keep pan and oil on stovetop over medium heat.

Lightly salt the chicken, then dip it one piece at a time into the cold rice batter, holding on to the tip with your fingers. Gently toss the chicken into the hot oil away from your body. Continue the process with more chicken pieces (about 6 to 8 pieces, depending on the size of your pan). Do not overcrowd. The temperature of the oil will lower as you add pieces of chicken. Using a slotted spoon or metal tongs, flip the chicken once to brown the other side. When both sides are browned, set on a tray or plate and continue battering and frying all the chicken. Between each batch, using the slotted spoon, scoop up any bits of batter left in the oil. You may have to add more coconut oil through the process. Always wait until the oil is hot enough before adding new batches of chicken.

To serve, sprinkle chicken with salt and pepper to taste, chili flakes, crispy garlic, cilantro, and scallion.

BARBECUE-INSPIRED CHICKEN PIZZA

Everyday •• Omnivore

Take an American favorite—barbecue—and add it to another American favorite—pizza—and what's not to love? This recipe keeps it simple and uses the all-natural ingredients of our homemade Ketchup for the sauce to avoid the harmful effects of overprocessed and sweetened bottled barbecue sauce. This also makes it easier and faster to prepare. It's a great way to use up leftover chicken too.

Makes 1 large pizza

> **1 recipe Gluten-Free Pizza Dough (page 60)**
>
> **1 tablespoon cornmeal**
>
> **½ to ¾ cup Ketchup (page 66)**
>
> **1 chicken breast, precooked and cut into bite-size pieces**
>
> **¼ sweet potato, cut into very thin half rounds**
>
> **½ cup finely diced broccoli**
>
> **2 thin rounds of red onion, cut in half**
>
> **¼ cup grated mozzarella cheese**
>
> **½ cup grated gouda cheese**

Preheat oven to 450°F.

Cover a cutting board with a piece of parchment paper. Using a rolling pin, roll out pizza dough into a large circle approximately ⅛ inch thick. Because this dough uses gluten-free flour and no refined flour at all, it doesn't have the same malleability as your usual pizza dough. Be careful not to tear it.

Sprinkle a large oven tray with the cornmeal. Carefully lay the pizza dough on top of the cornmeal, turning edges up to create a border. Spread the ketchup over the pizza crust, and then lay the chicken pieces over the sauce. Top with sweet potato rounds, broccoli, and onion slices. Sprinkle with cheeses.

Bake for 12 to 15 minutes, until the top has just melted and the crust has been cooked through. Slice and serve warm.

MEDITERRANEAN VEGGIE PIZZA

Everyday •• Vegetarian

When it's pizza night at our house, this version is Margaret's favorite. It's light and zesty, and switching out the typical tomato sauce with pesto makes it a little different from your usual pizza fare.

Makes 1 large pizza

> **1 recipe Gluten-Free Pizza Dough (page 60)**
>
> **1 tablespoon cornmeal**
>
> **½ to ¾ cup Pumpkin-Seed Vegan Pesto (page 151)**
>
> **1 cup spinach**
>
> **1 portobello mushroom, thinly sliced lengthwise**
>
> **2 to 3 tablespoons sun-dried tomatoes**
>
> **½ cup crumbled goat or sheep feta**

Preheat oven to 450°F.

Cover a cutting board with a piece of parchment paper. Using a rolling pin, roll out pizza dough into a large circle approximately ⅛ inch thick. Because this dough uses gluten-free flour and no refined flour at all, it doesn't have the same malleability as your usual pizza dough. Be careful not to tear it.

Sprinkle a large oven tray with the cornmeal. Carefully lay the pizza dough on top of the cornmeal, turning edges up to create a border. Spread the pesto over the pizza crust, and then lay the spinach over the sauce. Top with mushrooms, then sun-dried tomatoes, and sprinkle with feta cheese.

Bake for 12 to 15 minutes, until top has just melted and the crust has been cooked through. Slice and serve warm.

Note about sun-dried tomatoes: We prefer to get our sun-dried tomatoes dry, not packed in any oil. If your sun-dried tomatoes are extremely hard, you'll need to reconstitute them by soaking them in warm water for 10 to 15 minutes. If they're a little soft and chewy, you can use them as is, without reconstituting.

SALAMI PIZZA

Everyday •• Omnivore

James grew up eating pizza every Friday night, as part of a family tradition. Even though he doesn't eat it often these days, pizza—in particular salami pizza—still ranks high on his list of favorite comfort foods. This version adds some green in the form of kale to up the vegetable content.

Makes 1 large pizza

- 1 recipe Gluten-Free Pizza Dough (page 60)
- 1 tablespoon cornmeal
- ½ to ¾ cup Marinara Sauce (page 142)
- 2 cups stemmed and finely shredded kale
- 4 to 6 ounces shredded mozzarella cheese
- 3 to 4 ounces nitrate-free salami, cut into thin rounds
- 3 tablespoons grated Parmesan cheese

Preheat oven to 450°F.

Cover a cutting board with a piece of parchment paper. Using a rolling pin, roll out pizza dough into a large circle approximately ⅛ inch thick. Because this dough uses gluten-free flour and no refined flour at all, it doesn't have the same malleability as your usual pizza dough. Be careful not to tear it.

Sprinkle a large oven tray with the cornmeal. Carefully lay the pizza dough on top of the cornmeal, turning edges up to create a border. Spoon the Marinara Sauce over the pizza crust, and then spread 1 cup of the kale over the sauce. Sprinkle the mozzarella cheese over the kale, then place the rounds of salami on top of the cheese. Spread the rest of the kale over the salami and top with Parmesan cheese.

Bake for 12 to 15 minutes, until top has just melted and the crust has been cooked through. Slice and serve warm.

NUT-CRUSTED PESTO CHICKEN

Impress the neighbors •• Omnivore

Even though this recipe is in the "impress the neighbors category," it's actually quite simple to make, and the return for your investment of time is sheer deliciousness. If you've got the pesto already made, the time required drops significantly and qualifies this as an "everyday" recipe. Serve with a side of sautéed veggies like broccoli, zucchini, and bell peppers.

Makes 4 servings

4 chicken breasts, cut in half to equal thickness

½ cup Pumpkin-Seed Vegan Pesto (page 151)

1½ cups Nut Crust (page 42)

1 teaspoon ghee or butter

5 cloves garlic, cut into thin rounds

2 carrots, grated (about 1 cup)

2 tablespoons thinly sliced sun-dried tomatoes

2 cups baby spinach

2 tablespoons thinly sliced fresh basil

Preheat oven to 395°F.

In a large bowl, coat chicken breasts with pesto. Pour ½ cup of the Nut Crust into a separate dish. Dredge each chicken breast in the Nut Crust until fully covered, and place on oven tray. Repeat until all chicken is coated. Bake chicken for 10 to 12 minutes until cooked through.

While chicken is baking, heat ghee or butter in a medium pan over medium heat. Add the garlic rounds, carrots, and sun-dried tomatoes, and sauté for 2 minutes, until just heated. A little color in the garlic rounds is okay.

Divide the spinach evenly among four plates. Plate each chicken breast on the bed of spinach, using the sautéed vegetables as a garnish with a little fresh basil sprinkled on top.

Note about sun-dried tomatoes: We prefer to get our sun-dried tomatoes dry, not packed in any oil. If your sun-dried tomatoes are extremely hard, you'll need to reconstitute them by soaking them in warm water for 10 to 15 minutes. If they're a little soft and chewy, you can use them as is, without reconstituting.

ASIAN ROASTED CHICKEN

Impress the neighbors •• Omnivore •• Make it once, use it lots

This recipe gives an Asian twist to our favorite roasted chicken recipe (which we included in *Eat Naked*). It's guaranteed to be juicy and tender, and oh so flavorful. It takes some time to make, but most of that time is unattended. The yield is very large, and definitely worth the wait.

Since you've already got the oven on, this pairs nicely with some additional roasted veggies, or a nice big salad works too. Use the leftovers in salads for lunches.

Makes 6 to 8 servings

- 1 small roaster chicken (approximately 3 to 4 pounds)
- 1 tablespoon unrefined coconut oil
- 1 tablespoon gluten-free tamari soy sauce
- 1 teaspoon store-bought or homemade Mustard (page 67)
- 1 lemongrass stalk
- 2 limes, quartered
- 4 shallots, peeled and sliced
- ½ small daikon radish, peeled and coarsely chopped into bite-size pieces (approximately 1 cup)
- 1 large sweet potato, cut into ½-inch half moons
- 2-inch piece fresh ginger, cut into 4 rounds
- 1½ cups filtered water
- ½ cup store-bought or homemade Coconut Milk (page 44) (optional)
- 1 bunch bok choy, coarsely chopped (3 to 4 cups)

Preheat oven to 385°F. While oven is preheating, clean the chicken and remove and set aside any organs that may be inside. (Organs can be used for making stock, along with the chicken bones after roasting.) Whisk together coconut oil, tamari, and mustard into a paste and rub all over the outside and inside of the chicken.

Cut the lemongrass stalk into 1- to 2-inch pieces, cut in half lengthwise. Stuff half of the lemongrass stalks, half of the lime wedges, and all shallots inside the bird. Put 2 lime wedges between the skin and the meat at the top of the breast. Place the chicken in a roasting pan, with the daikon radish, sweet potato, ginger, and the rest of the lemongrass and lime spread around it.

Combine coconut milk with 1½ cups filtered water, and pour into the roasting pan around the chicken. Cover and roast for about an hour, depending on the size of the bird. Remove cover and continue to bake for another 15 minutes, or until a meat thermometer inserted into the chicken reads 165°F. Add the bok choy, spreading it around the sides of the chicken, and cook for another 15 minutes. The chicken should be nicely browned.

Remove from oven and let stand for 10 minutes to cool slightly before serving. Slice chicken into parts and serve warm, spooning some of the vegetables onto each plate alongside it.

PESTO VEGETABLE LINGUINI

Impress the neighbors •• Vegetarian, with vegan option •• Better than naked

This recipe is a great one for those who can't do gluten and are avoiding the starch of pasta. It uses broccoli stems, zucchini, and butternut squash sliced into long thin strips to resemble linguini. This technique is easiest if you have a mandoline, which will make quick work of slicing the veggies. Cutting it all by hand is possible, but quite a lot of work. Even though we've included this recipe in the "impress the neighbors" category, if you're speedy with the mandoline, it won't take much time. The slicing is the most labor-intensive part.

Feel free to add your favorite protein to this meal, like chicken or shrimp. Just cook separately and add to the large bowl with vegetables before adding pesto. For a vegan version of this recipe, substitute olive oil for ghee.

Makes 4 servings

- 2 to 3 heads broccoli, chopped (into bite-size florets), long stems reserved (about 2½ cups florets and 2 to 3 stems)
- 2 zucchini, ends removed
- 1 small butternut squash, peeled, halved, and seeded
- 1 teaspoon ghee or extra-virgin olive oil
- ½ cup sun-dried tomatoes, thinly cut on the diagonal
- 4 cloves garlic, minced
- Sea salt
- Freshly ground pepper
- 2 cups stemmed and finely chopped lacinto kale (other kale varieties okay)
- ½ to ¾ cup Pumpkin-Seed Vegan Pesto (page 151)
- 2 tablespoons pumpkin seeds, preferably presoaked and dehydrated or slow-roasted (optional)
- 1 tablespoon thinly sliced basil leaves
- 1 teaspoon chili flakes (optional)

Using a mandoline, slice the long broccoli stems, zucchini, and butternut squash into long thin strips, to resemble linguini, until you have approximately 2½ cups of each vegetable. In a large skillet, heat a teaspoon of ghee over medium heat. Add the linguini-like vegetables and lightly sauté for 2 minutes, then add sun-dried tomatoes, broccoli florets, and garlic, and cover pan for 2 to 3 minutes. Remove from heat when broccoli is bright green and other vegetables are still al dente. Place in a large bowl and season with salt and pepper to taste. Add kale to bowl with vegetables while they are still hot and mix well. The residual heat will cook the kale without overcooking it.

Add pesto to vegetables in bowl and mix to coat. Plate and garnish with pumpkin seeds, basil, and chili flakes.

Note about sun-dried tomatoes: We prefer to get our sun-dried tomatoes dry, not packed in any oil. If your sun-dried tomatoes are extremely hard, you'll need to reconstitute them by soaking them in warm water for 10 to 15 minutes. If they're a little soft and chewy, you can use them as is, without reconstituting.

NOODLE-LESS LASAGNA

Impress the neighbors •• Omnivore

This recipe replaces noodles with thin slices of vegetables: zucchini, yellow crooked-neck squash, and eggplant. Cut thin enough, they don't require precooking and add more vegetables to a dish that is typically mostly noodles, meat, and cheese. Plus, they do a remarkable job of mimicking the texture of the pasta you're used to. We've also added onions, mushrooms, and kale to the meat mixture to pack in even more veggie power. This dish is easiest to make if you have a mandoline. It's doable without one but will require more time and better knife skills.

Makes 6 to 8 servings

- 1 tablespoon butter or ghee
- 1 onion, cut into ¼-inch dice
- 1 teaspoon sea salt
- 8 ounces crimini or white mushrooms, cut in half lengthwise and then thinly sliced
- 1 pound ground grass-fed beef (can substitute ground bison as well)
- 2 heaping teaspoons dried oregano
- 1 clove garlic, thinly sliced
- 1 cup stemmed and finely chopped kale
- 1 recipe Marinara Sauce (page 142)
- 1 eggplant, cut lengthwise into strips as thin as possible
- 2 zucchini, cut lengthwise into strips as thin as possible
- 1½ cups ricotta cheese
- 2 yellow crooked-neck squash, cut lengthwise into strips as thin as possible
- 8 ounces mozzarella cheese, grated

Preheat oven to 395°F.

In a large skillet, heat butter over medium heat. While butter is heating, prepare vegetables. Sauté onions, adding ½ teaspoon of the salt, for 3 to 5 minutes, until just translucent. Add mushrooms and sauté for another 3 to 5 minutes or until soft. Add ground beef, remaining ½ teaspoon salt, oregano, garlic, and kale, stir to combine, and cook for 5 to 10 minutes. Meat will still be slightly undercooked.

To assemble lasagna, spread ½ to ¾ cup of Marinara Sauce on bottom of a 10½-inch-by-13 ¼-inch-deep lasagna pan. Cover with one layer of eggplant slices, placed lengthwise, and then one layer of zucchini slices, placed crosswise. Spread ¾ cup of the ricotta cheese on top of zucchini layer, and put ½ to ¾ cup of Marinara Sauce over the cheese. Next add a layer of yellow squash, placed lengthwise, the opposite direction of the zucchini.

Put the ground beef, onion, and mushroom mixture over the yellow squash. Pour another ½ to ¾ cup of Marinara Sauce over the beef. Place another layer of yellow squash on top of the Marinara Sauce in the same direction, lengthwise, as you did the last layer. Spread the remaining ricotta cheese on top of the yellow squash, with another ½ to ¾ cup of Marinara Sauce on top of the cheese. Place a layer of zucchini crosswise on top of the sauce, with the final layer of eggplant placed lengthwise on top of the zucchini.

Pour remaining sauce over eggplant, using a flexible spatula to spread it out evenly. Sprinkle grated mozzarella cheese over the lasagna. Cover with aluminum foil and bake, covered, for 30 to 40 minutes, until eggplant is cooked through. Remove foil, and bake for another 10 minutes, to brown the top. Remove from oven and let sit for 3 to 5 minutes before slicing and serving.

ZESTY PULLED BEEF

Impress the neighbors •• Omnivore

This recipe is another one that takes time to make, but most of that time is unattended. Cooking the beef slowly makes it nice and tender. We've made sure to keep the vegetable content up by serving it over kale. This recipe goes well with any roasted veggies, such as Roasted Asparagus (page 114) or Roasted Brussels Sprouts (page 115).

Makes 4 servings

- 1 tablespoon ghee
- 1 onion, sliced (approximately 1 cup)
- ½ teaspoon sea salt
- 2 stalks celery, cubed (approximately 1 cup)
- 1 red bell pepper, diced (approximately 1 cup)
- 2 (14.5-ounce) cans diced fire-roasted tomatoes
- 1 cup dry full-bodied red wine, such as Cabernet Sauvignon
- 2 cups Beef Bone Broth (page 49) or water
- 1 pound beef (chuck roast, rump roast, or top round—something boneless), left whole or cut in half to fit in pan
- 1 bunch kale, stemmed and chopped (approximately 4 cups)

In a large saucepan, heat ghee over medium heat. Brown the beef, about 2 minutes each side, and set aside. Add onions to pan and sauté, adding sea salt, for 2 to 3 minutes, until just soft. Add celery and red bell pepper, and sauté for 2 minutes.

Add the tomatoes, red wine, broth, and beef. Cover and bring to a boil over medium heat. Once boiling, reduce heat to low and allow to simmer for 1 hour. Uncover the pot and continue simmering for another 30 minutes. Meat is done when it easily pulls when stuck with a fork.

Remove the meat from the pan, leaving the juices in the pan on the stovetop, and bring to a boil. Turn the heat to high and reduce the sauce for 10 to 15 minutes, until thick. Let meat cool slightly and, using a fork, pull the beef into shreds. This should happen easily, as the meat should be thoroughly cooked by now.

Put the meat back in the sauce, and serve over raw kale. The heat from the beef will lightly steam the kale as it sits.

ROAST BEEF

Impress the neighbors •• Omnivore

Roast beef is the ultimate meal for a Sunday-night family dinner. When Margaret was growing up, her grandmother would make roasts every week—such a great tradition.

We like to make a roast of some sort about once every other week. One of the benefits of a roast is that you typically end up with far more meat than you need, which gives you leftovers to be used in creative ways throughout the rest of the week. A roast is our solution for sandwich meat, which, when store-bought, is one of those foods often laden with salt, additional flavorings, and preservatives. Leftover roast beef is a truly naked alternative.

We've created this recipe using a very small roast. If you're cooking for larger numbers of people, you may need to double the amount of the rub. Estimate ½ to ⅔ pound of meat per person and this will give you ample meat for leftovers.

Makes 4 servings

   2 teaspoons store-bought or homemade Mustard (page 67)

   ½ teaspoon sea salt

   ½ teaspoon dried or fresh thyme

   ½ teaspoon paprika

   ½ teaspoon granulated garlic

   2 to 3 pounds beef roast (rump or tri tip works best)

Create a rub by mixing the mustard, sea salt, thyme, paprika, and granulated garlic into a paste. Rub all sides of the meat with the paste. Let sit at room temperature for 30 minutes, marinating in the rub.

Preheat oven to 300°F. Set a wire rack on an oven tray or in a shallow roasting pan, and set the roast on top of the wire rack. If there's a layer of fat on the meat, put that side on top. Insert a meat thermometer as it's cooking. Roast for 1 to 1½ hours, until meat thermometer reads 130°F to 140°F for a medium-rare roast, or 145°F to 150°F for medium. Remove from heat and allow to sit for 3 to 5 minutes before slicing.

TURKEY MEATBALLS

Impress the neighbors •• Omnivore •• Better than naked

Turkey meatballs are notorious for being dry and kind of tasteless. Not ours. These are moist and super-yummy. Also, gluten often hides in meatballs in the form of breadcrumbs added to keep them moist. In this recipe, we substitute zucchini and walnuts for the bread, which have a similar effect on the meatball without the gluten. Serve with Marinara Sauce (page 142) or with Pesto Vegetable Linguini (page 190).

Makes approximately 30 meatballs

2 tablespoons ghee

1 small onion, diced (approximately ½ cup)

1 zucchini, grated (approximately 1 cup)

4 mushrooms, diced (approximately ½ cup)

1 teaspoon paprika

1 teaspoon dried oregano

1 teaspoon granulated garlic

½ teaspoon ground cumin

1 teaspoon dried thyme

½ pound ground turkey, white meat

½ pound ground turkey, dark meat

½ teaspoon sea salt

½ cup walnuts, preferably presoaked and dehydrated or slow-roasted

1 tablespoon parsley

Preheat oven to 395°F.

Heat 1 tablespoon of the ghee in large skillet over medium heat. Add onions to pan and sauté lightly for 2 to 3 minutes to soften them. Add zucchini and mushrooms to pan, and sauté for another 2 to 3 minutes, until soft. Add paprika, oregano, granulated garlic, cumin, and thyme. Stir to mix well and remove from heat.

In a large bowl, mix turkey with vegetable and spice mixture and sea salt. Stir to mix well. In a food processor, combine walnuts and parsley, and pulse until finely minced. Add to turkey mixture and stir well.

Heat the rest of the ghee in a large skillet over medium heat. Mold turkey mixture into tablespoon-sized balls, making sure they are equally sized so that they cook evenly. Drop the meatballs onto skillet to brown, rolling them periodically to make sure they brown evenly all around, about 1 minute per position. Use a metal spatula to ensure you get a clean turn, and don't leave any browned bits stuck to the pan. As they brown, remove them from pan and place on an oven tray. When all meatballs have been browned and put on the oven tray, bake for 10 to 15 minutes, until cooked through.

SWEET POTATO SHEPHERD'S PIE

Impress the neighbors •• Omnivore, with vegetarian option

This is our version of the traditional shepherd's pie. Instead of mashed potatoes, it uses the less-starchy Sweet Potato Mash or Roasted Cauliflower Mash. It also ups the veggies significantly and makes sure not to overcook them. This is a delicious meal for a cold winter's night—hearty and warming. To make a vegetarian version, substitute kidney beans for the ground beef.

Makes 6 servings

> 1 teaspoon ghee
>
> ½ red onion, cut into ¼-inch dice (approximately ½ cup)
>
> ½ teaspoon sea salt
>
> 2 celery sticks, cut into ¼-inch dice (approximately ½ cup)
>
> ¼ teaspoon chili powder
>
> 1 teaspoon paprika
>
> 2 tablespoons thyme
>
> 1 pound ground grass-fed beef or ground turkey, or 2 cups presoaked and precooked kidney beans
>
> 1 cup chopped (into ½-inch pieces) green beans
>
> 1 (14.5-ounce) can of no-sodium diced tomatoes
>
> 1 recipe Sweet Potato Mash (page 112) or Roasted Cauliflower Mash (page 113)

Heat the ghee in a large skillet over medium heat. Sauté onion with salt for 2 minutes, until just translucent. Add celery, chili powder, paprika, thyme, and mix well. Add ground beef and stir to mix. Chop the green beans and add them to the meat as it cooks. Add tomatoes and mix well. Let cook for 3 to 4 more minutes, or until meat is cooked through.

Spread the meat mixture into an 8-inch-by-8-inch pan. Using a spatula, press down so that there are no air bubbles. Spread the Sweet Potato Mash on top of the meat mixture, using a spatula to smooth out the top. If you're feeling fancy, you can make a little design on top using an icing bag.

Turn on the broiler to high and cook pie for 5 to 7 minutes, until top is a nice shade of brown. Remove from oven and let cool for a few minutes before slicing and serving warm.

Tip: To make a do-it-yourself piping bag, take a thick plastic storage bag and cut the corner off the bottom of it at an angle and width for what you want to decorate. Fill the bag with the topping and then roll the top of the bag to tighten and control the flow of ingredients out of the cut hole. If you have decorating tips, you can insert them into the hole and pipe shapes and designs.

QUINOA VEGETABLE SUSHI

Impress the neighbors •• Vegan •• Better than naked

Sushi is usually made with white, starchy rice. Our recipe uses high-protein, less-starchy Quinoa, which adds both nutritional value and a nutty flavor. We've kept this recipe vegan, but you can easily add some Seared Tuna (page 171) or smoked salmon in place of the avocado to up the protein content. Mirin is a sweet wine that can be found in most grocery stores, usually in the international or Asian section.

Makes 6 rolls of 8 pieces each

1 recipe Quinoa (page 54)

2 tablespoons apple cider vinegar

½ cup plus 1 tablespoon gluten-free tamari soy sauce

2 tablespoons mirin or 1 tablespoon raw honey

1 large carrot, peeled and julienned

1 small daikon radish, peeled and julienned

1 red bell pepper, seeded and julienned

1 cucumber, peeled, seeded, and julienned

1 avocado, thinly sliced

Juice of 1 lime (approximately 2 tablespoons)

6 sheets nori seaweed

2 cups spinach

1 teaspoon grated fresh ginger

1 tablespoon chopped scallions

1 tablespoon chopped cilantro

Prepare the grain as described in the recipe for Quinoa. While Quinoa is cooking, in a large bowl, mix together the apple cider vinegar, 1 tablespoon of the tamari, and mirin. Next, prepare the vegetables.

Put the carrot, cucumber, daikon, and bell pepper into the bowl with the tamari marinade and mix well. Let vegetables marinate for 30 minutes. In a separate small bowl, combine the avocado slices with the lime juice to prevent the avocado from browning.

When the Quinoa has been cooked, remove it from the heat and spread it out on an oven tray, leaving it at room temperature to cool.

Wet a dishtowel and wring it as dry as you can with your hands. Lay it out on a cutting board. Lay 1 sheet of nori on top of the damp towel, shiny side up. Spread ½ cup of the cooked and cooled Quinoa on the bottom half of the nori paper, leaving ½ inch along the bottom of the nori free of quinoa.

Cover the quinoa with 7 to 10 spinach leaves. Starting from the bottom, lay out the marinated julienned vegetables in rows starting with carrot, then cucumber, then daikon, then red bell pepper, using about 2 sticks of each vegetable. Add 1 row of avocado slices (or tuna or salmon) on top of the julienned vegetables.

Starting at the bottom where all of the vegetables are, roll up the nori sheet toward the opposite end, keeping it as tight as you can. Wet the very top edge of the sheet of nori to stick it to the roll (visit www.eatnakednow.com/videos for a video demonstration of this technique). Once you have it in a roll, slice it crosswise into 8 pieces. It's easiest to start by cutting the roll into 2 equal halves, and then cutting each half into 4 pieces each.

Repeat with remaining pieces of nori and vegetables. Plate and serve at room temperature, or refrigerate with a lightly dampened towel over the rolls for no longer than 24 hours to prevent them from drying out.

In a small bowl, make a dipping sauce by combining ¼ cup water, the remaining tamari, ginger, scallions, and cilantro. Stir to mix well.

CEVICHE CHORONI

Impress the neighbors •• Pescatarian •• Raw

This recipe comes from Jorge Gonzalez, the father of one of James's closest college friends. Jorge made the recipe one night in the beautiful town of Choroni on the central coast of Venezuela. He made the ceviche with grouper he'd caught fresh and ingredients he'd hand-picked that same day. Talk about naked! This is a slightly modified version of his original recipe.

Ceviche uses the acidity of lemon and lime juice to "cook" the fish, killing any possible pathogens without the damaging effects of heat. Traditionally this dish is made with a sweet pepper found in Latin America and the Caribbean called the *ají dulce* pepper, which translates to "sweet chili." It's related to the habanero pepper but is sweet. Unless you're a local to these regions, these peppers can be difficult to find, so we recommend using any sweet pepper. Serve with Raw Kale and Cabbage Salad (page 105) to make a full and entirely raw meal. *¡Buen provecho!*

Makes 4 servings

¼ **cup freshly squeezed lemon juice**

½ **cup freshly squeezed lime juice**

½ **cup finely diced red onion**

½ **cup finely diced white onion**

½ **cup finely diced sweet peppers, any variety and multiple colors if possible**

1 **garlic clove, minced (approximately ¼ teaspoon)**

½ **teaspoon sea salt**

¼ **teaspoon freshly ground black pepper**

10 **ounces boneless red snapper, sea bass, or young grouper**

¼ **cup coarsely chopped cilantro**

1 **young green coconut at room temperature**

1 **teaspoon red pepper flakes (optional)**

In a small bowl, combine lemon juice, lime juice, onions, sweet peppers, garlic, salt, and black pepper. Stir to mix, and let sit on counter for 10 minutes for the flavors to gel. While flavors are melding, cut the fish into 1-inch cubes.

Add the chopped fish and the cilantro to the bowl with the juice and other veggies, pressing the fish down into the bowl to make sure the lemon and lime juice is covering it. Chill, covered, in the refrigerator for 2 hours, checking periodically to ensure the fish is still covered by the lime and lemon juice, which is "cooking" it. Strain the lemon and lime juice from the fish, reserving it in a small dish.

Using a large knife, open the young green coconut (visit www.eatnakednow.com/videos for a video demonstration of this technique). Pour the coconut water into a large glass bowl. Using a spoon, following the circumference of the shell and pressing firmly, strip the coconut meat away from the shell. You may still get slivers of shell stuck to the coconut meat. Just pull them off with your fingers. Cut the coconut meat into small thin slices, and add to the fish. Add 1 cup of the coconut water and stir to combine all ingredients well.

Serve in chilled cocktail glasses and garnish with red pepper flakes to add some spiciness. The strained lemon/lime juice can be served alongside the ceviche in a small bowl as a side for dipping if you like it a little more lemony.

12
Sweet and Savory Snacks

Snacks are another one of those foods that often have all sorts of un-naked ingredients in them when you buy them commercially. A bag of potato chips, a muffin from the coffee shop, a chocolate bar: sugar, salt, artificial fats. Take your pick (or rather, don't!). The good news is that it doesn't have to be that way.

We reach for snacks because we're short on time, on the go, in a rush. The main obstacle is usually time. That's why the key to success with making your own healthy snacks is a little planning—and some creativity. You'll want to plan ahead in one of two ways (or both): Make snacks on the weekend for the week ahead, or make sure your kitchen is stocked with enough naked ingredients that you can throw together a snack quickly.

Many of the snacks in this section are grab and go, requiring a little advance prep but very little time to assemble. Many use the "make it once, use it lots" approach that's ideal for snacks. Some can double as appetizers.

CUCUMBER-WRAPPED BEEF

In a rush •• Omnivore

This recipe makes use of leftover beef of any type and wraps it in a thin slice of cucumber. It sounds fancier than it is, and like some of the other savory snacks, it can be used as an appetizer for a posh dinner as easily as something to munch on in the midafternoon. This recipe is much easier and goes faster if you have a mandoline. If you don't have one, consider switching it up and making more of a stack by cutting the cucumber in little rounds: Place a slice on the bottom, then a dab of dressing, then a little piece of beef and some minced green onion on top if you're feeling fancy.

Makes 10 to 12 mini-wraps, depending on size of cucumber

1 long cucumber

Your favorite salad dressing (see "Sauces, Dressings, and Dips" chapter for ideas)

Leftover cooked grass-fed beef, cut into 1-inch lengths approximately ¼ inch thick (steak, roast, whatever you have on hand)

1 scallion, cut into 1-inch pieces

Using a mandoline or a very sharp knife, slice the cucumber lengthwise as thinly as possible. You'll know the cucumber is sliced too thick if you try to roll the slice and it either breaks or won't stay wrapped. Spread approximately 1 teaspoon of dressing onto the cucumber. Put a piece of beef and a length of scallion at one end of the cucumber and then roll it up. Repeat with the remaining pieces of cucumber. Plate and serve cold or at room temperature.

Tip: If your wraps aren't staying rolled, you can use long thin slices of the green part of the scallion to tie the wrap together.

SAVORY STOVETOP POPCORN

In a rush •• Vegetarian, with vegan option

Why use microwave popcorn with all those weird flavorings, colorings, and artificial ingredients when the real thing takes so little time? This recipe takes about 5 minutes and is incredibly flavorful. Note that it uses ghee—clarified butter—rather than the cheap and overrefined vegetable oils so commonly used. Experiment with different spices to suit your personal taste. This combination is our household favorite. For a vegan version of this popcorn, replace the ghee and butter with coconut oil.

Makes 2 to 4 servings

   1 tablespoon ghee or unrefined coconut oil

   ½ cup organic popcorn kernels

   1 tablespoon butter or coconut oil

   1 tablespoon nutritional yeast

   ¼ teaspoon chili powder

   1 teaspoon oregano

   ¼ teaspoon freshly ground pepper

   ½ teaspoon sea salt

   ¼ teaspoon paprika

   ¼ teaspoon granulated garlic

Melt ghee in 5-quart pot over medium heat. Put 2 popcorn kernels in the ghee and cover the pot. When the kernels pop, the ghee is hot enough to make popcorn. Add the rest of the popcorn, cover, and leave on heat for about 3 minutes, until popping has subsided. If you leave it for too long, the popcorn will burn, so don't go far from the stove! A good trick is to shake the pot using oven mitts, and listen to determine whether there are a lot of kernels left.

Remove pot from heat, pouring popcorn into a big bowl. Put the butter into the pot you used to make the popcorn, and let it melt from the residual heat. As the butter is melting, mix together the nutritional yeast, chili powder, oregano, pepper, salt, paprika, and granulated garlic in a small bowl.

Toss popcorn with melted butter and sprinkle with the spice mixture. Pairs really nicely with your sweetie and a movie rental.

CHEESE QUESADILLA

In a rush •• Vegetarian •• Better than naked

This is a great example of a light meal that doesn't take a lot of planning and that makes use of miscellaneous things you probably already have in your fridge. Use any type of cheese you have on hand and any type of sprouts or greens. Unlike most quesadillas, it uses a sprouted corn tortilla instead of wheat. These are available at most health food stores. If you can't find sprouted corn tortillas, use regular corn tortillas—but make sure the ingredients are only the basics: corn, water, lime, and sea salt.

Also, you'll notice that these quesadillas are more heavy on the greens than the cheese. That's intentional and our way of sneaking more vegetables in wherever we can.

Makes 1 quesadilla

1 small sprouted corn tortilla

2 tablespoons cheese (cheddar, chèvre, mozzarella, whatever you have on hand)

2 to 3 tablespoons Cultured Salsa (page 68) or Spicy Salsa Verde (page 70)

½ cup sprouts (clover, alfalfa, sunflower, or any type you like) or greens (arugula or spinach)

Heat a small skillet over medium heat. Put tortilla in the pan (no oil), and crumble or grate the cheese over top. Add the salsa, and when cheese has melted (takes only 2 to 3 minutes), add the sprouts or greens. Fold the tortilla in half and serve warm.

AVOCADO SPROUT NORI WRAPS

In a rush •• Vegan •• Raw

This recipe is easy and fast, and makes great use of something most people don't get enough of in their diets: sea vegetables. Sea vegetables are a natural and abundant source of lots of important minerals, including trace minerals we don't get easily elsewhere. This wrap is a sheet of nori seaweed (the type that's usually used for sushi) filled with avocado and sprouts. It's generous with the greens, has a little fat to keep you satiated until your next meal, and is easy to grab when you're on the go.

Makes 1 wrap, or 4 to 6 pieces of sushi

> **1 sheet nori seaweed**
>
> **½ cup sprouts (clover, alfalfa, sunflower, whatever your preference)**
>
> **½ avocado, flesh scooped out**
>
> **Wedge of lime**
>
> **Gluten-free tamari soy sauce, for dipping (optional)**

Wet a dishtowel and wring it as dry as you can with your hands. Lay it out on a cutting board. Lay the sheet of nori on top of the damp towel, shiny side up. Place sprouts over the bottom half of the nori, and then spread spoonfuls of avocado on top of the sprouts. Squeeze the lime wedge over the sprouts and avocado.

Starting at the bottom where the sprouts and avocado are, roll up the nori sheet toward the opposite end, keeping it as tight as you can. Wet the very top edge of the sheet of nori with a little water to stick it to the roll (visit www.eatnakednow.com/videos for a video demonstration of the technique).

Once you have it in a roll, slice it crosswise into 8 pieces. It's easiest to start by cutting the roll into 2 equal halves, and then cut each half into 4 pieces each.

Dip in tamari and enjoy!

Tip: A sharp knife is best when slicing these rolls. If you're having trouble, wet the blade of your knife before slicing, to ensure clean cuts.

CAPRESE STACKS

In a rush •• Vegetarian

This is a play on the Italian caprese salad, which uses a soft unripened mozzarella cheese (such as bocconcini), tomatoes, and basil. Instead of putting these in a salad, you create little stacks. They're fast and easy to make, and impressive enough to use as an appetizer for guests.

Makes 1 serving

1 tomato, sliced into 4 thick rounds

Sea salt

4 big basil leaves

4 (¼-½ inch thick) slices of unripened mozzarella cheese

1 teaspoon balsamic vinegar (a high-quality, thick balsamic works really nicely here if you have one)

Lay the tomato rounds on a plate, sprinkle with a dash of sea salt, and lay a basil leaf on top of each. Put the cheese rounds on top of the basil and drizzle with balsamic vinegar. Serve immediately.

MIXED FRUIT AND NUTS WITH COCONUT BUTTER

In a rush •• Vegan •• Better than naked

This recipe is one that James makes for his personal-chef clients and is met with rave reviews. It's incredibly simple and really delicious, particularly when berries are in season. You can mix it up and use whatever fresh fruit you like, but our favorite is berries.

Makes 1 serving

- ½ cup mixed fresh berries (whatever's in season and looking good at the market)
- 1 tablespoon chopped nuts, preferably presoaked and dehydrated or slow-roasted (pecans, almonds, walnuts, cashews, whatever you have on hand)
- 1 heaping tablespoon Raw Coconut Butter (page 51)
- Pinch cinnamon (approximately ¼ teaspoon)

Mix together the berries and nuts in a bowl. Add spoonful of coconut butter on top and sprinkle with cinnamon. Enjoy!

ALMOST-RAW ROCKET SHAKE

In a rush •• Vegetarian •• Better than naked

This is a healthier, mostly raw version of a tasty shake made at a local diner here in Los Angeles. The only ingredient that isn't raw is the coffee.

To keep this recipe as raw as possible, we recommend using raw milk and a raw egg. In both of these cases, the quality of the ingredients is paramount. If you're not able to source clean raw milk from healthy, grass-fed cows, then organic pasteurized milk is your next best option, and if you're not able to source eggs from healthy, pastured chickens, then skip them.

Makes 3 (8-ounce) servings

1½ cups raw whole milk from grass-fed cows

¼ cup espresso, cooled, or ½ cup coffee, cooled

1 egg from pastured chicken

1 heaping tablespoon raw cacao powder

2 tablespoons raw honey

¼ cup presoaked raw almonds (these don't need to be dehydrated) or 2 tablespoons almond butter

6 to 8 ice cubes (the more ice cubes, the thicker the shake)

Combine all ingredients in a high-powered blender, and blend on high until smooth (you may need to pulse a few times to make sure the ice has been crushed fully). Drink immediately while it's cold.

CELERY STICKS WITH CULTURED CREAM CHEESE

In a rush •• Vegetarian, with vegan option •• Better than naked

This is a slight variation on the classic "ants on a log" snack your mom might have made for you as a child (celery sticks with peanut butter and raisins). Instead of peanut butter, it uses the Cultured Cream Cheese that's a by-product of making Whey, and instead of raisins, you sprinkle the cheese with a pinch of dill. Quick, easy, and delicious. For a vegan version, replace the cheese with almond butter and skip the dill.

Makes 2 servings

> ¼ **cup Cultured Cream Cheese (page 63)**
>
> **2 long stalks celery, cut into 4-inch-long pieces**
>
> **Dash dried dill**

Spread the cream cheese in the wedge of the celery sticks, and sprinkle with dried dill. Enjoy!

COCONUT CREAMSICLE BITES

Everyday •• Vegan •• Better than naked •• Make it once, use it lots

Who didn't grow up loving Creamsicle ice cream bars from the ice cream truck? For many of us, those flavors of cream and orange are stuck in our taste buds since childhood. This is a quick and healthy sweet snack that brings those two flavors back again, in a simple, gluten-free, and low-sugar format.

Makes about 30 bites

> ¾ **cup shredded, unsweetened coconut**
>
> **1 cup whole rolled gluten-free oats**
>
> **1 cup whole cashews, preferably presoaked and dehydrated or slow-roasted**
>
> ¼ **cup raw sunflower seeds, preferably presoaked and dehydrated or slow-roasted**
>
> **1 cup pitted dates (about 10 dates)**
>
> **2 oranges, zested and juiced**

Place ¼ cup of the coconut on a plate and set aside.

Place the rolled oats in a heavy-bottomed skillet and toast for a few minutes over medium heat, stirring constantly. When they begin to turn a darker shade of tan at the edges and emit a toasted aroma, transfer the oats to a food processor. Pulse on high to pulverize them into a fine meal.

Add the remaining ½ cup coconut, cashews, and sunflower seeds to the food processor, and blend to finely chop them. Add the dates, orange zest, and half of the orange juice, and blend until the ingredients come together to form a homogeneous mass. Add a bit more orange juice, if needed, to get the right thickness and well-blended consistency. Don't add too much juice; you want the mixture to be fairly dry, not moist and mushy.

Use your hands to form the mixture into tablespoon-sized balls about 1 inch in diameter, then roll the balls in the reserved shredded coconut. Place on a plate and chill for an hour or so in the freezer before serving.

GRAINLESS GRANOLA BARS

Everyday •• Vegan •• Better than naked •• Make it once, use it lots

Like our Grainless Granola (page 88), these granola bars bypass the problem of gluten altogether by being made primarily of nuts and seeds, with some dried fruit. We've used natural, unprocessed sugar—and a lot less of it than you'll find in conventional granola bars. These make great to-go snacks or even a dessert if paired with some Coconut Ice Cream (page 232).

Makes 25 to 30 bars

2 cups almonds, preferably presoaked and dehydrated or slow-roasted

1 cup sunflower seeds, preferably presoaked and dehydrated or slow-roasted

¾ cup dried unsweetened and unsulphured cherries or dried fruit of choice

¼ cup whole flaxseeds

¼ cup ground flaxseeds

¼ cup ground hemp seeds

Meat from 1 young green coconut (approximately ½ cup packed) or ½ cup dried coconut flakes (unsweetened)

¼ cup pitted dates

¼ cup grade B or C maple syrup

¼ teaspoon sea salt

½ teaspoon cinnamon

½ teaspoon grated fresh ginger

Preheat the oven to 350°F.

While oven is heating, combine all ingredients except for ¼ cup of the dried cherries in a food processor and pulse repeatedly until they're well mixed and attain a granola-like consistency. Turn out the contents of the food processor into a bowl, add the remaining ¼ cup of dried cherries, and mix with a spoon.

Line an oven tray with parchment paper and pour the granola onto the tray. Using wet hands or a moistened rolling pin, press the granola into a square of the desired thickness (we recommend ¼ inch thick).

Bake for 10 minutes to just harden. Remove from the oven and use a knife to score the granola sheet into strips 1 inch by 2 inches long. Put it back in the oven and bake for another 10 minutes, until slightly brown. Remove from oven and let cool for 5 to 10 minutes. Using spatula, remove from the oven tray and set out on a cooling rack to finish cooling. Store in a covered glass container in the freezer. They're good for up to 2 months.

RUSTIC VEGAN MUFFINS

Everyday •• Vegan •• Make it once, use it lots

So often gluten-free muffins are dense and hard, and vegan muffins tend to be dry. These muffins are low in sugar, gluten-free, dairy-free, egg-free, and yet surprisingly light and moist. For easy cleanup, we recommend that you use muffin-tin liners. This recipe uses teff flour, which is a whole-grain, gluten-free flour found at most health food stores or online. Teff is a staple of the Ethiopian diet and the grain used to make their famous injera bread. Go to the "Resources" section of www.eatnaked.com for suggested brands and where to buy it.

Also, you can make your own almond flour by simply grinding almonds—even better: soaked and dehydrated almonds—in a food processor until they achieve a flour consistency. All the more naked!

Makes 12 muffins

 1 cup almond flour

 ½ cup teff flour

 ½ cup sorghum flour

 ½ teaspoon baking soda

 ½ teaspoon baking powder

 1 teaspoon cinnamon

 1 teaspoon vanilla extract

 1 tablespoon ground flaxseed

 ¼ cup maple syrup

 Zest and juice from 1 lemon (approximately 1 tablespoon zest and 2 to 3 tablespoons lemon)

 ½ cup store-bought or homemade Coconut Milk (page 44)

 2 tablespoon unrefined coconut oil

 ½ cup fresh (whatever is in season and flavorful) or frozen berries

Preheat oven to 350°F.

Mix almond flour, teff flour, sorghum flour, baking soda, baking powder, and cinnamon in a medium bowl. In a separate large bowl, mix together the vanilla, ground flaxseed, maple syrup, lemon zest and juice, and coconut milk. Mix well.

Gently fold the dry ingredients into the wet ingredients and mix well. Fold in the berries last. Evenly distribute the batter among 12 large muffin tins, either greased with a little coconut oil or lined with muffin liners.

Bake for 12 to 15 minutes. Check the muffins at 12 minutes with the toothpick test: stick a toothpick in the muffin and if it comes out dry, they're done. If it comes out wet, then leave it for another 3 to 4 minutes.

Let cool and enjoy! These muffins are best eaten when fresh, but if necessary, you can freeze them in a container for up to 1 month.

GARDEN VEGETABLE SCONES

Everyday •• Vegetarian •• Make it once, use it lots

These savory scones are an excellent midafternoon snack, especially nice with some fresh Cultured Butter. Once made, they're also a nice portable snack for any time during the week.

Makes 8 scones

1 cup sorghum flour

1 cup gluten-free oat flour

2 teaspoons baking powder

½ teaspoon sea salt

1 tablespoon finely chopped fresh dill

1 tablespoon dried thyme

¾ cup grated sharp cheddar cheese

¼ cup cold store-bought or homemade Butter (page 64)

1 cup store-bought or homemade Yogurt (page 65)

2 tablespoons shredded carrot

2 tablespoons grated zucchini

1 tablespoon thinly sliced sun-dried tomatoes

1 tablespoon finely chopped green onion, both green and white parts

Preheat oven to 350°F. While oven is heating, make the batter: In a large bowl, mix together the sorghum flour, oat flour, baking powder, sea salt, dill, thyme, and cheese. Stir together using a fork. Using a knife, cut butter into ¼-inch cubes. Add into flour mixture and use your hands to crumble it into the flour. The consistency should be like sand. If you have a pastry cutter, you can use that to mix the butter into the flour.

Add the yogurt, carrot, zucchini, sun-dried tomatoes, and green onion to the flour mixture, mixing lightly with a spatula. Lightly flour a large cutting board with sorghum flour. Knead the dough using your hands until well mixed. Form dough into a ball, and then press it onto the floured cutting board into a round approximately 1 inch thick.

Cut the round into wedges, kind of like a pie cut into 8 pieces. Separate the pieces and lay on an oven tray lined with parchment paper. Bake for 15 to 20 minutes, until scones bounce back when you press gently on them with your finger and are lightly browned on the bottom.

Note: We've specified gluten-free oat flour in this and a few other recipes. Oats themselves don't contain gluten, but they're often processed in facilities that also process gluten-containing grains, and so cross-contamination risk is extremely high. An oat flour that was processed with no risk of contamination will specify that on the label. Otherwise, assume that any oat flour (or any oat product for that matter) is contaminated with gluten.

CHEESY VEGAN KALE CHIPS

Impress the neighbors •• Vegan •• Better than naked •• Make it once, use it lots

Kale chips are a favorite of ours. They're crispy like potato chips, but without all the excess salt and refined oils. And, of course, they're a great way to get more green into your diet. In *Eat Naked*, we included a very basic recipe for making kale chips. Here we've upped the fancy-factor a little, adding nut "cheese" and some nice seasonings.

Because we're using olive oil and we're mimicking the effects of a dehydrator with the oven by cooking at quite a low temperature, these chips take a long time. Luckily, they don't require much work from you once they're in the oven.

We're using the oven for this recipe, but if you'd like to keep the chips raw and you have a dehydrator, follow the directions up until putting them on the oven trays. Put the kale on the trays that go into your dehydrator, set the dehydrator to 115°F, and let dehydrate for 8 to 10 hours, until crispy.

Makes 6 to 8 cups

2 big bunches kale

½ small red onion, thinly sliced

1 cup cashews, preferably presoaked and dehydrated or slow-roasted

1 tablespoon nutritional yeast

½ teaspoon chili powder

¼ teaspoon ground cumin

½ teaspoon ground turmeric

½ teaspoon sea salt

1 clove garlic, peeled

Juice of ½ lime (approximately 2 teaspoons)

3 tablespoons extra-virgin olive oil

¼ teaspoon freshly ground pepper

1 teaspoon paprika

Preheat oven to 250°F.

Wash and stem the kale. Rough chop the leaves into chip-size pieces. Toss in a large mixing bowl with red onion and set aside.

In a food processor, combine cashews, nutritional yeast, chili powder, cumin, turmeric, sea salt, garlic, lime, and olive oil. Pulse until mixture becomes a fine paste. Add ¼–½ cup of filtered water 1 tablespoon at a time and continue to blend until the mixture is the consistency of cheese sauce. Keep adding water until you reach the desired consistency.

Pour the cashew "cheese" sauce over the kale and onions, and mix well to coat the kale. You don't have to cover all of it equally, but do make sure there's some sauce on all the leaves. Lay the kale mixture out on a couple of oven trays and bake for 2½ to 3 hours, until crispy. Pull chips out of oven and turn every 45 minutes to ensure they're cooking evenly.

When chips are crispy, pull out of oven to cool. Sprinkle with paprika and serve warm. You can also store them in a covered container. They won't be quite as crispy after sitting for a while, but you can pop them into the oven briefly to crisp them up again.

ZESTY CRACKERS

Impress the neighbors •• Vegan •• Better than naked •• Make it once, use it lots

Crackers are one of those snack foods that are loaded with un-naked and overprocessed ingredients like refined flour, sugar, trans fats, and too much salt. These crackers take a little effort but are so delicious they're worth putting in a little elbow grease.

We've given instructions for making the crackers in the oven, but if you have a dehydrator, you can use that instead and keep them raw. Simply lay the sheet of uncut crackers on a dehydrator tray and dehydrate them at 108°F for 12 to 20 hours, until mostly dry. Remove from dehydrator and cut into desired shapes. Return the cut crackers to the dehydrator tray without the parchment paper and dehydrate for another 1 to 2 hours, until nice and crispy.

Makes 45 to 50 crackers

¼ **red onion, coarsely chopped (approximately ¼ cup)**

1 **cup almonds, presoaked and dehydrated or slow-roasted**

½ **cup hulled sunflower seeds, soaked (these don't need to be dehydrated)**

¼ **cup flaxseed, brown or golden**

1 **tablespoon dried oregano**

1 **tablespoon coarsely chopped sun-dried tomato**

½ **teaspoon sea salt**

½ **teaspoon red pepper flakes (optional)**

1 **zucchini, grated (approximately 1 cup)**

Preheat oven to 350°F.

Combine all ingredients in a food processor. Pulse several times until mixture forms a slightly gritty paste.

Lay a piece of parchment paper on your countertop and put the veggie-seed mixture on it. With the bottom of a spatula or a wet rolling pin, flatten the veggie and seed mixture into a sheet approximately ⅛ inch thick. Do your best to make it of an even thickness. Slide the parchment paper onto an oven tray and bake for 20 minutes.

Remove pan from oven and score the sheet with a knife or a small cookie cutter into the shapes you want the crackers to be. You're not cutting them at this point, you're just indenting. Put the scored crackers back in the oven for another 7 to 10 minutes, until nice and crispy.

Remove from oven and let cool. Separate crackers from each other along lines you scored earlier. Once crackers have cooled completely, store them in a covered container. If storing for more than a week, keep them in the fridge to maintain freshness. Otherwise, they'll last for about a week. Save the crumbs and other leftover bits, store them in a container, and sprinkle them over your next salad.

SEA CRACKERS

Impress the neighbors •• Vegan •• Better than naked •• Make it once, use it lots

These crackers have been named after a superfood included in them: sea vegetables (a fancy name for seaweed). Sea vegetables are high in minerals, particularly trace minerals that are vital to our health but not commonly found in our diet. This recipe makes use of two types of seaweed: dulse and nori. Dulse is essentially a sea lettuce, and nori is made using a combination of different seaweeds that are shredded and dried in sheets. Nori is commonly used as wrapping in sushi rolls. You can find both of these at Asian markets, health food stores, and some grocery stores.

We've given instructions for making these crackers in your oven, but if you have a food dehydrator, you can make a completely raw version. Simply lay the sheet of uncut crackers on a dehydrator tray and dehydrate them at 108°F for 12 to 20 hours, until mostly dry. Remove from dehydrator and cut into desired shapes. Return the cut crackers to the dehydrator tray without the parchment paper, and dehydrate for another 1 to 2 hours, until nice and crispy.

Makes 30 to 35 crackers

½ cup flaxseeds, brown or golden

½ cup hulled sunflower seeds, soaked (these don't need to be dehydrated)

½ cup sesame seeds

¼ cup cashews, preferably presoaked and dehydrated or slow-roasted

¼ cup dulse

1 sheet nori seaweed

1 clove garlic, peeled and grated

1 teaspoon grated fresh ginger (or 1 teaspoon dried)

Zest of 1 lime

½ teaspoon sea salt

¼ cup packed cilantro

½ teaspoon coriander seeds

2 pitted dates

1 large carrot, grated (approximately 1 cup)

Combine all ingredients in a food processor. Pulse several times until mixture forms a slightly gritty paste.

Lay a piece of parchment paper on your countertop and put the veggie-seed mixture on it. With the bottom of a spatula or a wet rolling pin, flatten the veggie and seed mixture into a sheet approximately ⅛ inch thick. Do your best to make it of an even thickness. Slide the parchment paper onto an oven tray and bake for 20 minutes.

Remove pan from oven, and score the sheet with a knife or a small cookie cutter into the shapes you want the crackers to be. You're not cutting them at this point, you're just indenting. Put the scored crackers back in the oven for another 7 to 10 minutes, until nice and crispy.

Remove from oven and let cool. Separate crackers from each other along lines you scored earlier. Once crackers have cooled completely, store them in a covered container. If storing for more than a week keep them in the fridge to maintain freshness. Otherwise, they'll last for about a week. Save the crumbs and leftover bits, store them in a container, and sprinkle them over your next salad.

THAI VEGETABLE COLLARD ROLLS

Impress the neighbors •• Vegan •• Make it once, use it lots

These are much like Thai summer rolls, but we've used the more nutrient-dense collard green leaves as a wrapper instead of rice paper. These make a nice fancy appetizer for a party, or make them on the weekend and use them as a snack throughout the week.

Makes 8 to 10 rolls

8 to 10 collard green leaves

3 ounces thin rice noodles

½ red bell pepper, julienned (approximately ½ cup)

1 carrot, julienned (approximately ½ cup)

1 small cucumber, julienned (approximately ½ cup)

20 basil leaves

Few sprigs mint

½ cup Thai Peanut Sauce (page 147)

Bring 4 cups of water to a boil in a large saucepan. Dip the collard green leaves into the hot water for 10 seconds, or until just softened. Using tongs, remove from the water and lay out on a tray to cool. Turn off heat and put rice noodles into hot water. Let sit for 7 to 10 minutes, until water has been absorbed.

To assemble the rolls, lay out a collard leaf with its backside facing up, stem on the bottom. Using a sharp knife, slice along each side of the stem and remove the stem, leaving the top part of the leaf attached. Lay 1 to 2 pieces of basil and mint on the collard leaf and then spread about ¼ cup of noodles across the lower third of the leaf, then lay 4 pieces of red pepper, 4 pieces of cucumber, and 6 pieces of carrot on top of the noodles. You may need to adjust the quantities somewhat based on the size of the leaf.

Starting at the bottom, fold the bottom edge of the leaf up and over the fillings. Fold both sides in, then roll up tightly (visit www.eatnakednow.com/videos for a video demonstration of this technique). Serve with Peanut Sauce for dipping, or store, refrigerated, until ready to eat. You can cut each wrap in half crosswise for presentation if you like.

RAW DAIKON-WRAPPED TUNA ROLLS

Impress the neighbors •• Pescatarian, with vegan option •• Raw

This recipe is sure to impress. These rolls are beautiful and absolutely delicious. The tricky part is mastering the assembly, but once you've made this snack a couple of times, you'll be a pro. Since you'll want the veggie strips to be wide, thin, and long, shop for sizable vegetables. For a vegan version, omit the tuna and increase the amount of avocado.

Makes 10 to 12 mini-rolls

- **1 large carrot**
- **1 daikon radish**
- **1 English cucumber, washed but not peeled**
- **¼ cup raw unfiltered apple cider vinegar**
- **4 tablespoons gluten-free tamari soy sauce**
- **¼ pound sushi-grade ahi tuna**
- **½ cup baby spinach**
- **½ avocado, thinly sliced**

Using a vegetable peeler, peel the carrot, daikon radish, and cucumber into long thin strips. Use an even pressure with the vegetable peeler so that the strips come out the same thickness over their whole length. If you have a mandoline, you could use this instead. (You'll know if the vegetables are sliced too thick if you try to roll the strip and it either breaks or won't stay rolled.)

Put vegetable peels into a medium bowl and mix with apple cider vinegar and 2 tablespoons of tamari. Mix well to ensure the vegetables are coated with the vinegar and tamari. Set aside to marinate for 20 minutes or less. While veggies are marinating, cut the tuna and avocado into thin slices.

To assemble, lay out 1 strip of daikon radish on a cutting board. Put 2 to 3 leaves of spinach on top of the radish, then 1 strip of cucumber, a strip of carrot, two small pieces of tuna, and a slice of avocado. Line up all the ingredients so that they're aligned lengthwise on top of the daikon radish. If they are different widths, line them up with one side of the radish creating a flat bottom. Make sure the daikon is the longest of all the veggies because it's acting as the wrap. Roll the vegetables as tightly as possible, forming mini sushi-style rolls.

Serve with remaining tamari as you would sushi.

Tip: Lay the paper wrapping from your fish or meat over your cutting board, and cut the fish or meat on top of it. This helps prevent cross-contamination of your cutting boards and makes cleanup easier.

13
Desserts

We believe desserts are a wonderful special-occasion food. Not something for every day, but a sweet treat to celebrate something special.

All of our dessert recipes use natural sweeteners and not too much of them. One of the sweeteners we like is coconut sugar, which is a naturally produced, low-glycemic sweetener that can be found at most health food stores. (Go to the "Resources" section at www.eatnakednow.com for more information on natural sweeteners and where you can buy them.) If you've got a mean sweet tooth, you might find some of these recipes not quite sugary enough. What we'd recommend is that you take a full week off of sugar, and then try one of these recipes. You'll find they're perfectly sweet, and your body will thank you for the respite from sugar.

As with our other recipes, we've made these gluten-free with a very specific intention to prove that gluten-free and healthy doesn't have to mean tasteless and dry.

CHOCOLATE MOUSSE

In a rush •• Vegan •• Better than naked

This creamy mousse is really easy to make and absolutely delicious. It stands easily on its own, or you can make it into individual tarts using the recipe for Vegan Piecrust (page 240). This is a particularly high-calorie dessert, using coconut and cashews. We recommend keeping portion sizes small.

Makes 2½ to 3 cups

1 (14-ounce) can regular full-fat coconut milk or ¾ cup plus 2 tablespoons homemade Coconut Milk (page 44)

1 cup dairy-free dark chocolate chips

1 cup presoaked cashews (these don't have to be dehydrated or slow-roasted)

Pour coconut milk into a small saucepan over low heat. Add chocolate chips and mix continuously as the chocolate melts, to keep the chocolate on the bottom of the pan from burning. As soon as the chocolate melts, remove from heat.

In a high-powered blender combine the chocolate mixture with the presoaked cashews. Purée until fully blended (you don't want it to be bitty), and pour into a serving dish. Chill in the refrigerator until ready to serve.

CREAM CHEESE ICING

In a rush •• Vegetarian

Our cream cheese icing is made naked by using raw honey in place of the usual highly refined icing sugar, and we've kept the sweetness to a minimum, recognizing that this icing is going to be used on cakes and cupcakes that are already sweet in their own right. We recommend using raw honey rather than pasteurized honey to get the full nutritional benefits. This icing is perfect for Carrot Cake (page 242) or Chocolate Cupcakes (page 244).

Makes approximately 2 cups

> 8 ounces organic cream cheese at room temperature
>
> ½ cup butter, softened
>
> 1 tablespoon vanilla extract
>
> 5 tablespoons raw honey
>
> Pinch sea salt

Combine all ingredients in a large bowl and use either a stand-up mixer or handheld blender to blend. Mix well. Use immediately or store in a covered glass container in the fridge for up to a week.

Tip: Use a piping bag, found at any baking supply store, to create professional-looking designs on your baked goods.

COCONUT ICE CREAM

Everyday •• Vegan •• Raw

Cold treats are delicious on a summer's day, but store-bought ice cream, even the "healthy" brands, still has too much sugar and all sorts of fillers. This recipe is a nice alternative because it satisfies that hankering for something creamy, cold, and sweet without leaving you with ice-cream gut afterward. It's dairy-free and soy-free, so it's good for those with food sensitivities. We use a blender to make it, rather than an ice-cream maker.

Makes 4 servings

> 1 (14-ounce) can coconut milk or ¾ cup plus 2 tablespoons homemade Coconut Milk (page 44)
>
> 1 teaspoon vanilla extract
>
> 2 tablespoons raw honey or 6 pitted dates
>
> ½ avocado, flesh scooped out
>
> ¼ cup cashews, presoaked
>
> 12 ice cubes (whole ice tray)

Put all ingredients except ice cubes in a high-powered blender and blend until creamy. Add ice cubes and blend until smooth.

Let cool in freezer to harden for up to 3 hours, and then eat. Don't leave it in the freezer for longer than 3 hours, as it will become very hard and difficult to scoop.

MARZIPAN COOKIES

Everyday •• Vegan •• Better than naked •• Make it once, use it lots

These cookies are simple, high in protein, flourless, and significantly lower in sugar than most marzipan. The almonds take a little time to soak but, otherwise, these are quite easy to make.

Makes 18 to 20 cookies

> 2½ cups almonds, soaked overnight and peeled
>
> 1 tablespoon almond extract
>
> ½ cup coconut sugar

Preheat the oven to 350°F.

Drain the almonds, rinse them, and drain them again. Remove the almond skins by rubbing them with a clean, damp dishtowel. Discard the skins.

Put the almonds in a food processor together with the almond extract and coconut sugar, and pulse repeatedly until ground to a fine pulp. Add ⅛ to ¼ cup filtered water as needed to make a thick paste.

Line an oven tray with parchment paper and spoon out batter in 1-tablespoon rounds. These cookies don't expand, so as long as they're not touching each other, they'll be fine. Bake for 15 to 20 minutes, until just golden. Make sure not to let them get too brown on the bottom. Enjoy warm, or store in a sealed container in the freezer for up to 1 month.

Tip: If you find the dough to be a little too soft, simply stick it in the freezer for 20 to 30 minutes or so to harden it up before baking.

RAW CHOCOLATE FUDGE

Everyday •• Vegan •• Better than naked •• Make it once, use it lots

This fudge is a bake-less, gluten-free, vegan version that isn't sickly sweet. It uses the food processor and just five basic ingredients. We put this in the "everyday" category, but once you've made it a couple of times, this could easily be made in less than 10 minutes.

Makes approximately 70 bite-size squares

- **1 cup raw, shredded, unsweetened coconut**
- **1 cup almonds, soaked overnight and peeled**
- **½ cup raw cacao powder**
- **¼ teaspoon sea salt**
- **1 cup raw, pitted dates**

In a food processor, pulverize coconut, almonds, cacao, and sea salt. When fully pulverized, add dates and continue to blend until dates have been mixed thoroughly with the other ingredients. The ingredients will begin to clump and form a doughy mass.

Remove the dough from the food processor and put it on a nonstick surface—plastic wrap or parchment paper is good. Using your hands or a rolling pin, and a second piece of plastic wrap or parchment paper over the dough, roll out the dough so that it's approximately ½ inch thick. Remove top parchment paper and cut the dough into ½-inch squares with a knife.

Enjoy immediately, or freeze squares in a sealed container. If you need to freeze them in layers, put a piece of parchment paper between each layer so they don't stick to each other. Frozen, they'll last up to 1 month.

WARM SQUASH PUDDING

Everyday •• Vegetarian •• Better than naked

This is a great way to use leftover cooked spaghetti squash. If you need to cook the squash first, that puts the timing of this recipe in the "impress the neighbors" category.

Makes 4 servings

2 cups cooked spaghetti squash (approximately ½ small spaghetti squash)

4 eggs, at room temperature

1 teaspoon vanilla extract

½ cup coconut sugar

1 cup store-bought or homemade Coconut Milk (page 44)

1 teaspoon cinnamon

Pinch sea salt

1 teaspoon butter

½ cup blueberries

½ cup pecans, preferably presoaked and dehydrated or slow-roasted, and coarsely chopped (optional)

If you haven't already cooked the squash, preheat oven to 395°F. Cut the squash in half lengthwise, and scoop out the seeds. Put the squash on an oven tray, cut side up, and bake for 15 to 20 minutes, until it compresses slightly when you press into the sides. It's done when you can run a fork lengthwise along the flesh, and it separates into strings. Remove from oven and let cool while you're preparing the remaining ingredients.

Combine cooked spaghetti squash, eggs, vanilla extract, coconut sugar, coconut milk, cinnamon, and sea salt in a blender and purée until smooth. Grease the insides of 4 small soufflé dishes or ramekins with the butter, and transfer the contents of the blender into them, filling them about three-fourths full. Evenly distribute the blueberries among the 4 dishes, dropping them into the batter. Bake for 25 to 30 minutes, until a toothpick inserted into the pudding comes out clean. These puddings will come out of the oven nice and poufy but will immediately start to deflate. That's okay. Serve warm, garnished with pecans.

CHOCOLATE CHIP COOKIES

Everyday •• Vegetarian, with vegan options •• Better than naked •• Make it once, use it lots

One of the reasons gluten-free baking has a bad rap is that it often yields dry, slightly flavorless cookies. How disappointing to bite into something that looks so delicious, only to have it be dry and bland. We've made these chocolate chip cookies with the specific intent of disproving this reputation. They are delicious, chewy, and all the good things you expect of a chocolate chip cookie. The only things they're missing are the gluten, the refined sugar, and the overprocessed vegetable oils. We've included vegan options for the butter and eggs.

One of the ingredients is almond meal. You can make your own "better than naked" almond meal from presoaked and dehydrated or slow-roasted almonds. To make 1 cup of almond meal, simply put a generous cup of almonds into your food processor, and process until it achieves the consistency of flour. It takes only a minute or two.

Makes 25 to 28 cookies

> 1 cup almond meal
>
> 1 cup sorghum flour
>
> ½ teaspoon baking powder
>
> ½ teaspoon sea salt
>
> ¾ cup coconut sugar
>
> ½ cup softened butter or unrefined coconut oil
>
> 1½ teaspoons vanilla extract
>
> ¼ cup maple syrup, grade B or C
>
> 1 egg or 2 tablespoons Flax Egg (page 41)
>
> 1 cup semisweet chocolate chips
>
> ½ cup walnuts or pecans, presoaked and dehydrated or slow-roasted, and coarsely chopped (optional)

Preheat oven to 350°F.

In a large mixing bowl, combine almond meal, sorghum flour, baking powder, and sea salt. In a separate medium bowl use a hand-held mixer to mix together the coconut sugar with the softened butter or coconut oil. Add vanilla extract and maple syrup, and continue mixing until well blended. Add the egg and continue to blend.

Pour the wet ingredients into the bowl with the dry ingredients. Add the chocolate chips and nuts and, using a flexible spatula, mix the ingredients well.

Line an oven tray with a sheet of parchment paper. If the dough is too runny, put it in the freezer for 5 to 10 minutes to harden it. Spoon out the cookie dough into rounded tablespoon mounds approximately an inch apart. Bake for 10 minutes. Remove from oven and let sit for 5 minutes to cool before transferring to a cooling rack.

Store in a covered dish when fully cooled. For longer-term storage, store in a zip-top bag in the freezer. Will keep for up to 1 month frozen.

ASIAN PEAR STRAWBERRY DELIGHT

In a rush •• Vegan •• Raw

This is a fresh and delicious way to take advantage of strawberry season. When chilled ahead of time, the Asian pear and strawberries set each other off beautifully, and the simple touch of the lime and mint take it over the top. It's amazingly quick to make, and so light and flavorful. It tastes like spring!

Makes 4 servings

> 16 chilled strawberries, quartered
>
> 1 chilled Asian pear, peeled, cored, and cut into ½-inch dice
>
> 1 lime, zested and juiced
>
> 1 teaspoon balsamic vinegar
>
> 1 tablespoon lightly chopped fresh mint leaves (unpacked)

Combine strawberries and pear in a bowl. Sprinkle with lime zest and juice, vinegar, and mint leaves. Toss to mix, and enjoy. Best served cold.

PEANUT BUTTER COOKIES

Everyday •• Vegetarian, with vegan options •• Make it once, use it lots

This recipe is an absolute favorite around our house. In fact, some might argue that James used these cookies to woo Margaret in the early days of their relationship. Gluten-free cookies get a bad rap for being dry and tasteless. These moist, delicious cookies will open your mind to the possibilities of gluten-free baking.

Keep this recipe naked by using peanut butter that has only peanuts on its ingredient list—no added sugar or oils. To spice it up even further, add ½ teaspoon cardamom or 1 teaspoon lime zest.

For a vegan version of this recipe, substitute coconut oil for ghee and use Flax Egg for the egg.

Makes approximately 25 cookies

- ½ cup ghee or unrefined coconut oil, at room temperature
- 1 cup coconut sugar
- 1 cup smooth or crunchy peanut butter, unsalted
- 1 egg or 2 tablespoons Flax Egg (page 41), at room temperature
- 1 teaspoon vanilla extract
- 1 teaspoon lime zest (optional)
- ¼ cup sorghum flour
- ¾ cup garbanzo bean flour
- ½ teaspoon sea salt
- ½ teaspoon cardamom (optional)
- ¼ teaspoon baking soda

Preheat oven to 350°F.

In a large mixing bowl, combine ghee and coconut sugar, either by hand or with an electric mixer, stirring well for a wet-sand consistency. Add peanut butter and mix thoroughly, so that it's nice and creamy. Add the egg, vanilla, and lime zest (if using), and mix until egg is completely incorporated into batter.

In a separate medium bowl, combine sorghum flour, garbanzo bean flour, sea salt, cardamom, and baking soda. Mix well. Combine dry ingredients with wet ingredients, stirring well to mix thoroughly.

Using a tablespoon, scoop balls out of the cookie dough and put on an oven tray lined with parchment paper, approximately 1½ inches apart. Using the back side of a fork, press firmly into each ball of cookie dough to form the cross-hatch pattern so often associated with peanut butter cookies. To keep your fork from sticking, keep it clean by wetting it with water.

Bake for 12 to 15 minutes or until cookies have a little resistance when you press gently on them with your finger (uncooked cookies will sink in when you press on them). Remove from heat and let cool for 3 to 5 minutes. Transfer to cooling rack with spatula.

Eat warm (yum!), or once cool, store in a covered dish for up to 1 week if kept in a cool space or in the freezer for up to 1 month.

VEGAN PIECRUST

Everyday •• Vegan

This is a versatile piecrust that can be used for just about any pie—from sweet to savory, vegan to meat. And, as with our other recipes, we're on a mission to show that gluten-free doesn't have to mean tough and tasteless. Use it as a base for Chocolate Mousse (page 230), for Avocado Lime Tart (page 241), or anywhere you'd use a piecrust.

One of the ingredients is almond meal. You can make your own "better than naked" almond meal from presoaked and dehydrated or slow roasted almonds. To make 1 cup of almond meal, simply put a generous cup of almonds into your food processor, and process until it achieves the consistency of flour. It takes only a minute or two.

Makes 1 piecrust

> **1 cup sorghum flour**
>
> **½ cup brown rice flour**
>
> **½ cup almond meal**
>
> **½ teaspoon sea salt**
>
> **¼ cup plus 1 to 2 tablespoons unrefined coconut oil**
>
> **¼ cup coconut sugar**
>
> **1 teaspoon vanilla extract**

Preheat oven to 350°F.

Combine sorghum flour, rice flour, almond meal, and sea salt in a medium mixing bowl, using a whisk or fork to mix well.

In a separate small bowl, combine ¼ cup of the coconut oil with the coconut sugar using a spatula, mixing it until it is a paste-like consistency. The coconut oil doesn't need to be melted, but ideally will be a little soft (at room temperature). Add vanilla and 3 tablespoons filtered water, and continue mixing until well combined.

Add the oil mixture to the flour mixture, and mix well with the flexible spatula. If you like, you can use your hands. Mix until it is a moist ball of dough.

Use the remaining coconut oil to grease your pie plate or tart pan. Using your fingers, press the dough into the pie plate or tart pan, until it's approximately ⅛ inch thick. Using a fork, prick some holes in the bottom of the crust, so that there's an escape route for air as the crust bakes (otherwise the crust will puff up and crack). Bake for 12 to 15 minutes, until it has just started to brown on the edges and is firm to the touch.

Let cool for 7 to 10 minutes before adding filling.

AVOCADO LIME TART

Everyday •• Vegan

When you're eating a sweet treat, it's really important nutritionally to balance it out with good-quality fats. The fat reduces your body's sugar spike, which means you have less of an insulin response. This recipe makes use of avocados for their creaminess and fat content. It's like a very healthy key-lime pie without any of the additives or gelatin.

Makes 1 large or 6 small tarts

> 1 recipe Vegan Piecrust (page 240)
>
> 2 avocados
>
> Juice of 4 limes (approximately ¼ cup)
>
> Zest from 1 lime
>
> ¼ cup store-bought or homemade Coconut Milk (page 44)
>
> ¼ cup raw honey
>
> ⅛ teaspoon salt

If not already made, make the piecrust in 1 large or several small tart pans.

While the crust is baking, scoop the flesh from the avocados and into a food processor. Add the lime juice, zest, coconut milk, honey, and salt. Blend well, making sure the honey hasn't sunk to the bottom.

When the crust is cool, spoon the avocado lime filling into the crusts. Serve immediately, or refrigerate and serve chilled.

CARROT CAKE

Impress the neighbors •• Vegetarian •• Better than naked

We're not big cake people, but we do love a good carrot cake. This version is gluten-free and uses much less sugar than most cake recipes. It's such a delicious, moist treat, and people will never guess it's a healthier version of the original.

One of the ingredients is almond meal. You can make your own "better than naked" almond meal from presoaked and dehydrated or slow-roasted almonds. To make 1 cup of almond meal, simply put a generous cup of almonds into your food processor, and process until it achieves the consistency of flour. It takes only a minute or two.

Makes 1 (8-by-8-inch) cake

   1 cup almond meal

   1 cup gluten-free oat flour

   ½ cup teff flour

   2 teaspoons baking soda

   1 teaspoon baking powder

   1 tablespoon cinnamon

   ½ teaspoon ground allspice

   ½ teaspoon ground nutmeg

   ¼ teaspoon sea salt

   1 cup coconut sugar

   ½ cup butter, at room temperature

   1½ teaspoons vanilla

   2 eggs

   2 cups grated carrot

   ½ cup buttermilk

   1 teaspoon grated fresh ginger

   ½ cup walnuts or pecans, presoaked and dehydrated or slow-roasted, chopped

   1 teaspoon unrefined coconut oil

   1 recipe Cream Cheese Icing (page 231) (optional)

Preheat oven to 350°F.

Sift the oat flour, teff flour, almond meal, baking soda, baking powder, cinnamon, allspice, and nutmeg together into a large mixing bowl. If you don't have a sifter, use a whisk to stir briskly so that all dry ingredients mix well. Add salt and stir well.

In a separate medium mixing bowl, add coconut sugar to butter, and use a handheld or standup mixer to mix well. With the mixer still running, add the vanilla. Add eggs one at a time. We recommend cracking the eggs into a small separate bowl first to ensure no bits of shell make their way into the cake batter. Set aside the mixer and add the grated carrot, buttermilk, grated ginger, and walnuts into the bowl with the wet mixture. Stir with a spatula to combine well.

Pour all liquid ingredients into bowl with dry ingredients. Using a spatula, mix together the dry and wet ingredients to form a batter.

Grease an 8-inch cake pan with coconut oil, making sure to grease the sides well. Pour batter into greased pan, using the back of a spoon or a spatula to make sure the batter is spread evenly throughout the pan.

Bake for 45 to 50 minutes, until a toothpick inserted into the cake comes out clean. Remove from oven and let cool before topping with icing. Just the cake, naked, is also a tasty treat.

Note: We've specified gluten-free oat flour in this and a few other recipes. Oats themselves don't contain gluten, but they're often processed in facilities that also process gluten-containing grains, and so cross-contamination risk is extremely high. An oat flour that was processed with no risk of contamination will specify that on the label. Otherwise, assume that any oat flour (or any oat product for that matter) is contaminated with gluten.

CHOCOLATE CUPCAKES

Impress the neighbors •• Vegetarian •• Make it once, use it lots

On special occasions, there's really nothing like a good chocolate cupcake. The problem with many cupcakes is that they're loaded with gluten, refined sugar, and vegetable oils that aren't suitable for use at high temperatures. Our cupcakes use sorghum flour, almond meal, and oat flour in place of the usual wheat flour and are sweetened with coconut sugar. We've even found a way to squeeze in some veggies! The grated zucchini makes the cupcakes impossibly moist, and even the most avid vegetable-hater won't be able to detect their presence. In fact, James made some of these cupcakes for our gluten-free adult friends at our wedding, yet they were gobbled up immediately by all the kids!

You can make your own "better than naked" almond meal from presoaked and dehydrated or slow-roasted almonds. To make 1 cup of almond meal, simply put a generous cup of almonds into your food processor, and process until it achieves the consistency of flour. It takes only a minute or two.

If you're feeling fancy, top these cupcakes with Cream Cheese Icing.

Makes 20 cupcakes

> **1 cup sorghum flour**
>
> **½ cup almond meal**
>
> **½ cup gluten-free oat flour**
>
> **1 cup unsweetened cocoa powder**
>
> **1½ teaspoons baking soda**
>
> **1 teaspoon cinnamon**
>
> **½ teaspoon ground allspice**
>
> **½ teaspoon sea salt**
>
> **½ cup coconut sugar**
>
> **½ cup butter, at room temperature**
>
> **1 teaspoon vanilla extract**
>
> **¼ cup maple syrup, grade B or C**
>
> **2 eggs, at room temperature**
>
> **2 small zucchinis, grated (approximately 2 cups)**
>
> **½ cup buttermilk**

1 cup semisweet chocolate chips

1 recipe Cream Cheese Icing (page 231) (optional)

Preheat oven to 350°F.

Sift the sorghum flour, almond meal, oat flour, cocoa powder, baking soda, cinnamon, and allspice into a large mixing bowl. If you don't have a sifter, use a whisk to stir briskly so that all dry ingredients mix well. Add salt and stir well.

In a separate medium mixing bowl, add coconut sugar to melted butter, and use a handheld or stand mixer to mix well. Stir in the vanilla and maple syrup. Add eggs one at a time, mixing well. We recommend cracking the eggs into a small separate bowl first to ensure no bits of shell make their way into the cupcake batter. Add buttermilk, and continue to mix well. Set aside the mixer and add the grated zucchini and chocolate chips into this wet mixture and stir with a spatula to combine well.

Pour all liquid ingredients into bowl with dry ingredients. Using a spatula, mix together the dry and wet ingredients to form a batter. Pour ¼ cup batter each into muffin tins lined with paper baking cups. Bake for 20 minutes, or until a toothpick inserted into the cupcake comes out clean. Let cool before topping with icing.

Note: We've specified gluten-free oat flour in this and a few other recipes. Oats themselves don't contain gluten, but they're often processed in facilities that also process gluten-containing grains, and so cross-contamination risk is extremely high. An oat flour that was processed with no risk of contamination will specify that on the label. Otherwise, assume that any oat flour (or any oat product for that matter) is contaminated with gluten.

BERRY COBBLER

Everyday •• Vegan

This is a great summer dessert that makes excellent use of berry season. We use our Grainless Granola for the crust, which means you have leftover granola for breakfast another day. It goes particularly well with Coconut Ice Cream (page 232).

Makes 4 to 6 servings

4 cups mixed berries (use whatever is in season and looks good at the market)

Juice of 1 lemon

2 tablespoons maple syrup, grade B or C

½ teaspoon cinnamon

2½ cups Grainless Granola (page 88)

Preheat oven to 350°F.

Mix together berries, lemon juice, maple syrup, and cinnamon in a bowl. Set aside while you make the granola if you haven't made it yet. (Note: If you are making the granola now, you don't need to bake it before using it in this recipe.)

Sprinkle ½ cup of the granola on the bottom of an 8-inch-by-8-inch baking pan. Add the berry mixture and then top it with the remaining 2 cups of granola. Bake for 45 minutes, until nicely browned on top.

APPENDIX A
One-Week Naked Menus

Not sure what a week of cooking and eating naked would really look like? We've created two sample menu plans to give you a starting point. The first assumes that you cook every meal and that each meal is something different. Honestly, this is a best-case scenario and happens rarely, even at our house. But it gives you a good sense of how the meals build off of each other. You'll see we've included the most meal prep on Sunday, and used those elements (sauces and crackers) throughout the week in different ways.

The second assumes that you lead a busy life and don't want to be in the kitchen all that much. It builds in lots of leftovers and a couple of repeats. This is more what a week at our household looks like.

Use either of these menus as a guideline. You'll note we didn't include any meals out or any room for your 20 percent indulgence time (we like to follow the 80:20 rule—80 percent of the time we're very deliberate and careful with our eating; the other 20 percent we create space for indulgences, so that this is a lifestyle we can sustain), which would affect the week as well.

Cooking Naked for One Week—Best-Case Scenario

	SUN	MON	TUES	WED	THURS	FRI	SAT
BREAKFAST	Green Smoothie	Kitchen Sink Breakfast (use your leftovers from Sunday's dinner)	Huevos Rancheros	Fast and Easy Eggs and Greens	Sweet Potato Hash	Curried Egg Scramble	Apple Pancakes
LUNCH	Quinoa Tabouleh (with Lemon Tahini Dressing)	Caesar Salad	Mexican Salad (with Tomatillo Avocado Sauce)	Asian Fusion Salad (with Speedy Asian Dressing)	Omega-Rich Arugula Salad	Seaweed Salad (with Carrot Ginger Dressing)	Raw Kale and Cabbage Salad
DINNER	Noodle-less Lasagna (save some marinara sauce for Friday's dinner)	Asian Roasted Chicken (with enough leftover chicken for lunches)	Sesame-Crusted Salmon with Speedy Asian Dressing (save some for Wednesday's lunch)	Sautéed Chicken with Lemon and Herbs	Quick and Dirty Beef Stir-fry with Quinoa (save leftovers for Sunday's lunch)	Chicken Pizza (with marinara sauce from Sunday's dinner)	Maple Sage-Glazed Pork
SNACK(S)	Savory Stovetop Popcorn	Zesty Crackers, with Tomatillo Avocado Sauce	Curried Lentil Soup	Cheese Quesadilla	Almost-Raw Rocket Shake	Raw Daikon-Wrapped Tuna Roll	Caprese Stacks
PREP	Vegan Caesar Dressing Tomatillo Avocado Sauce Zesty Crackers Crispy Shiitake Faux Bacon	Curried Lentil Soup			Carrot Ginger Dressing (for stir-fry)	Lemon Tahini Dressing	

Cooking Naked for One Week—In a Hurry

	SUN	MON	TUES	WED	THURS	FRI	SAT
BREAKFAST	Portobello Eggs Benedict	Wake-Up Shake	Amaranth Porridge	Florentine Omelet with a Twist	Kitchen Sink Breakfast	Fast and Easy Eggs and Greens	Holiday Pumpkin Smoothie
LUNCH	Ceviche Choroni	Wild Rice Salad	Curried Lamb Stew	Speedy Green Salad (with chicken)	Watercress Salad with Seared Tuna	White Bean Leek Soup	Eggplant Basil Salad (use pesto from Friday's dinner)
DINNER	Curried Lamb Stew	Broiled Sardines, with Quinoa	Long Life Greens (with chicken)	Seared Tuna, with Hearty Miso Soup	Nut-Crusted Pesto Chicken (make extra bite-size for Friday's snack)	Pesto Vegetable Linguini	Teriyaki Beef with Wild Rice Salad (save some beef for Monday's snack)
SNACK(S)	Coconut Creamsicle Bites	Cucumber-Wrapped Beef	Ceviche Choroni	Coconut Creamsicle Bites	Hearty Miso Soup	Nut-Crusted Chicken Bites	Raw Cucumber Mint Soup
PREP	Make enough stew for Tuesday's lunch (save extra cerviche for Tuesday's snack)	Make enough Quinoa for Wednesday's dinner	Make extra chicken for Wednesday's lunch	Save some seared tuna for Thursday's lunch Save some soup for Thursday's snack	Make enough pesto for Friday's dinner and Saturday's lunch	Save some pesto for Saturday's lunch	Save some wild rice for Monday's lunch Teriyaki Sauce

APPENDIX B
Eat Naked Food Tables

Here's your quick guide to eating naked by food types. These tables were originally included in *Eat Naked: Unprocessed, Unpolluted, and Undressed Eating for a Healthier, Sexier You* and will give you an at-a-glance overview of what we mean by "naked" in each food category. For further definition and discussion of these topics, we recommend that you pick up a copy of *Eat Naked* for yourself.

Produce: Good, Better, Best	
Best	Local, in season, fresh, organic
Next best	Local, in season, fresh
Okay	Frozen and organic without the extras: no sauces, flavorings, additives, or preservatives
Steer Clear	Frozen with the extras, canned (except tomatoes), otherwise packaged and processed

Meat: Good, Better, Best		
	Poultry and Pork	**Ruminants**
Best	Pastured	Grass-finished or grass-fed
Next best	Organic	Organic
Okay	Free range	
Steer Clear	"Natural" or other	"Natural" or other

Dairy and Eggs: Good, Better, Best			
	Milk	**Other Dairy Products (Cheese, Yogurt)**	**Eggs**
Best	Grass-fed, raw, unhomogenized	Made from raw milk from grass-fed cows	From pastured chickens
Next best	Organic, pasteurized, unhomogenized	Made from organic, pasteurized milk	Organic, omega-3 enhanced or not
Okay	Organic, pasteurized cow's milk Unsweetened almond milk Unsweetened coconut milk Unsweetened hemp milk	Made from conventional whole milk, unflavored and unsweetened	From free-range chickens
Steer Clear	Conventional, low-fat or nonfat, or flavored cow's milk Milk substitutes	Made from conventional, low-fat or nonfat milk, sweetened, or flavored Made from milk substitutes	Extra-large or jumbo eggs "Natural" or other factory-farmed eggs Egg substitutes Liquid eggs Powdered eggs

A Quick Reference Guide to Naked Fats			
Type of fat	**Characteristics**	**Examples**	**Uses**

Saturated	Stable
	Solid at room
	    temperature
		Coconut oil
		Animal fats from
		    grass-fed animals
			Cooking and baking

Monounsaturated	Less stable
	Solid in the fridge,
	    liquid at room
	    temperature
		Olive oil
		Almonds and almond
		    oil
		Avocados and
		    avocado oil
		Pecans
		Cashews
		Peanuts and peanut
		    oil
		Macadamia nuts and
		    macadamia nut oil
			Cooking at very low
			    temperatures
			Cold in dressings or
			    on steamed veggies

Polyunsaturated	Least stable
	Liquid at room
	    temperature and in
	    the fridge
		Fish oils
		Seed oils
			Store in the
			    refrigerator
			Cold in dressings or
			    on steamed veggies
			Do not cook with
			    these!

Grains, Beans, Nuts, and Seeds: Good, Better, Best			
	Grains	**Beans**	**Nuts and Seeds**
Best	Whole, sprouted	Soaked and cooked Fermented soy	Soaked and dried
Next best	Whole	Canned, low sodium	Home roasted
Okay		Canned	Raw

Steer Clear	Cereals
	"Low-carb" bread
	    products
		Unfermented soy	Already roasted or
			    seasoned

Beverages, Sweeteners, and Condiments: Good, Better, Best			
	Beverages	Sweeteners	Condiments
Best	Water Herbal or green teas Naturally fermented beverages like kombucha	Raw honey Unsulphured blackstrap molasses Rapadura Maple syrup (grade B or C) Stevia Coconut sugar Dates	Homemade from naked ingredients
Next best	Sparkling mineral water Black tea Freshly juiced vegetable juice	Pasteurized honey Grade A maple syrup	Store-bought, with only naked ingredients on the label
Okay	Coffee (preferably organic, shade-grown; if decaf, then Swiss Water Process) Unpasteurized, fresh-squeezed fruit juice, in small amounts only	Agave (it has a low glycemic value but is highly refined with a high fructose content)	
Steer Clear	Soda pop of any type (diet or regular) Pasteurized juice	Refined sugar (includes "brown" sugar, which is still refined) Artificial sweeteners	Any condiments with high-fructose corn syrup, hydrogenated oils, soy, or ingredients you can't pronounce

References

Layton, D. W., K. T. Bogen, M. G. Knize, F. T. Hatch, V. M. Johnson, and J. S. Felton. 1995. Cancer risk of heterocyclic amines in cooked foods: An analysis and implications for research. *Carcinogenesis* 16(1):39–52.

Pitchford, P. 2002. *Healing with Whole Foods: Asian Traditions and Modern Wisdom.* Berkeley, CA: North Atlantic Books.

Vallejo, F., F. A. Tomas-Barberan, and C. Garcia-Viguera. 2003. Phenolic compound contents in edible parts of broccoli inflorescences after domestic cooking. *Journal of the Science of Food and Agriculture* 83(14):1511–16.

Vom Saal, F. S. 2009. *Bisphenol-A.* Working paper, Division of Biological Sciences, University of Missouri–Columbia, 2009. http://endocrinedisruptors.missouri.edu /pdfarticles/Bisphenol_A_References.doc.

Wisconsin Department of Health and Family Services. 2000. *Polycyclic Aromatic Hydrocarbons (PAHs) Fact Sheet.* www.dhs.wisconsin.gov/eh/chemfs/fs/pah.htm.

Margaret Floyd is the author of *Eat Naked: Unprocessed, Unpolluted, and Undressed Eating for a Healthier, Sexier You*. She received her nutritional therapy practitioner certification from the Nutritional Therapy Association, was certified as a holistic health counselor by the Institute of Integrative Nutrition, and as a certified healing foods specialist. She is also certified by the American Association of Drugless Practitioners. She has a thriving private practice in Los Angeles, CA. Floyd's work with clients is focused on shifting their diet to a naked diet through gradual changes to their lifestyle, cooking methods, shopping habits, and recipes. She shares her passion for food and good health by teaching her clients how to eat so that they can enjoy both. Visit her at www. eatnakednow.com

James Barry is a graduate of the National Gourmet Institute of Health and Culinary Arts in New York. He has worked as a private chef for celebrities and is founder of Wholesome2Go, a healthy high-quality food delivery company currently serving the Los Angeles area. He is certified as a nutritional consultant through the Global College of Natural Medicine and as a certified healing foods specialist.

Index

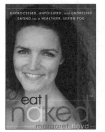
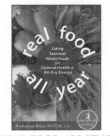

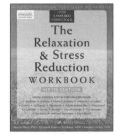